Praise for

Jan Coppola Bills & Late Bloomer

"Reading this is like having Jan right by your side in the garden. *Late Bloomer* is packed with ideas for making gardening easier and truly more enjoyable – nurturing advice and tips for late bloomers of any age! I love how Jan puts it: "Gardening is the art of soul to soil."

~ **Sue Goetz,** garden consultant, coach and designer, author of *The Herb Lover's Spa Book*

"Late bloomer gardeners understand the natural pace of the garden and appreciate all of its elements, from sun to rain, insects to birds, successes and learning opportunities, sometimes called failures or mistakes. Jan provides timely suggestions to guide us, all with an eye to not overdo, to take our time and enjoy all the experiences gardening has to offer."

~ **Jo Ellen Myers Sharp,** The Hoosier Gardener, editor at *State-by-State Gardening* magazines, author, speaker

"The best part of gardening at 60 is that I now know exactly what I want. I'm no longer lured by trends, especially high maintenance ones. Jan's *Late Bloomer* is spot on, sharing her wisdom for gardening in the second half of our gardening lives. Youth, too, can learn from Jan's wisdom. If I could travel back in time, I'd take this book with me. A must read for anyone wanting to simplify their lives."

~ **Helen Yoest,** Director, Bee Better, author of *Plants with Benefits* and *Good Berry, Bad Berry*

"Straight forward, easy to follow advice from a professional gardener who walks the walk. *Late Bloomer* incorporates knowledgeable tips delivered with a very personal touch."

~ **Pat Seibel,** Proven Winners® Display Garden Supervisor, Four Star Greenhouse, Inc.

"Sometimes, stepping back from years of gardening due to new physical limitations can be painful! But with the help of an experienced professional who listens to your needs and what you love most, you can STILL enjoy your gardens. Jan did just that for me. She designed and planted beds that can be managed and enjoyed for many years to come. The aging gardener will find many helpful tips in her new book."

~ **Anne Brant Hoyt,** client homeowner, southeastern MI

"People who embrace gardening later in life are the most avid gardeners I know! Jan Coppola Bills matches their enthusiasm with super garden ideas and wonderful photos. Her lively and engaging book is a must for those who are 'late bloomers' – and a great book for any garden lover."

~ **Jan Johnsen,** NY, Johnsen Landscape & Pools, author of *Heaven is a Garden*

"Aging gives us the opportunity to enjoy the simpler things in life. Gardens provide enjoyment and inner peace. Jan Bills' book, *Late Bloomer,* is filled with knowledgeable garden tips to help mature gardeners create an eye-pleasing and environmentally-safe garden. Sit back and enjoy the view!"

~ **Marie Churchill,** client homeowner, southeastern MI

LATE BLOOMER

LATE BLOOMER

How to Garden with Comfort, Ease and Simplicity in the Second Half of Life

JAN COPPOLA BILLS

St. Lynn's
press

PITTSBURGH

Late Bloomer

How to Garden with Comfort, Ease and Simplicity in the Second Half of Life

ISBN-13: 978-1-943366-05-7

Library of Congress Control Number: 2016938561
CIP information available upon request

First Edition, 2016

St. Lynn's Press . POB 18680 . Pittsburgh, PA 15236
412.381.9933 . www.stlynnspress.com

Book design – Holly Rosborough
Editor – Catherine Dees
Editorial Interns – Christina Gregory and Morgan Stout

Photo credits:
All photos © Jan Coppola Bills with the exception of the following:
Pages 12, 13, 14, 15, and 94 © Carla Carr; page 16 © Kylee Baumle; page 92 © Jenny Peterson, pages 93 and 117 © Jill Plumb; pages 17, 39 (both), 59, 72, 97, 98, 118 (both), 119 (top), 120 (bottom), 121 (top), 122 (bottom three), 124 and 137 © Holly Rosborough
Cover photo © Aly Darin Johnson-Hill

Printed in Canada
on certified FSC recycled paper using soy-based inks

This title and all of St. Lynn's Press books may be purchased for educational, business or sales promotional use. For information please write:
Special Markets Department . St. Lynn's Press . POB 18680 . Pittsburgh, PA 15236

10 9 8 7 6 5 4 3 2 1

To my darling brother

Michael

who lives forever
in my heart.

Table of Contents

INTRODUCTION

≈

Iam a second-half-of-life gardener. I truly believe that this is the time in life when we can experience our greatest gardening enjoyment. Maybe you are a second-halfer too, and that's why you've picked up this book. Or maybe you just want to tune into some words of hard-won wisdom from a gardener who has "been there," made mistakes, learned from them, and figured out what's really important and what's not – and evolved a way of gardening for the pure joy of it.

If you're curious to know what's so different about gardening in this "half," I'd say it's all about a shift in perspective. Instead of a drive to completion and outcome and control, it's now about a more deeply soul-pleasing way of gardening, defined by words like these:

- **Simplicity**
- **Beauty and Harmony**
- **Comfort and Ease**
- **Celebrating Life with Food from Your Soil**
- **Relaxation and Letting Go** (and not minding who's nibbling on your lettuce)

One of the many loads of mulch I've worked with!

I began gardening in 1991, when my husband and I purchased our first home. Yes, I am a late bloomer. I had no prior gardening history or experience, but that did not stop me. I adorned every inch of our love shack, season after season, with all the wrong plants in all the wrong places. I was that person who insisted that sun-loving plants would grow wonderfully in dense shade, and vice-versa. I spent tons of money at my favorite garden center each weekend and hauled in truckloads of compost and mulch. Clueless, I forged on until years later when I miraculously developed a deep spiritual connection with Mother Earth. I look back lovingly at those memorable (and hysterical) days gone by. I have learned a great deal since then about gardening and life, but will never forget how I got my roots!

Today, I garden for many different reasons and outcomes that extend beyond my personal needs and desires. This shift in thinking began after the sudden death of my brother, Michael, in 2006. To say that we had been close doesn't adequately describe our loving and mutually supportive relationship. His death shook me to the core and had a profound impact on my future. It was a call to deep evaluation of my path and goals. I asked myself, *What am I doing with my life? How much time do any of us have?* And, most importantly: *What will make me feel happy and fulfilled?*

Michael and me in the yard

The absence of my dear brother influenced me to switch careers and start Two Women and a Hoe®, do something I truly loved, and start a small gardening business in southeast Michigan. I replaced my corporate high heels for Wellies and never looked back. Each day I am blessed to mix business with pleasure. But more importantly, my true passion in this second half of life is to give more than I take – in and out of the garden. I am discovering that the fine art of gardening is ultimately giving back to the earth, wildlife, nature... and us. Gardening is the fine art of soul to soil. If there is a Late Bloomer's credo, it would go something like this:

- I will plant only what I can comfortably tend.
- I will not give myself tasks beyond my ability to easily achieve.
- I will ask for help, if necessary.
- I will not concern myself with "perfection."
- I will allow my garden to deepen my connection with nature.
- I will garden simply because it pleases my soul.

I believe the work of a gardener and an artist is synonymous: both create masterpieces with their hands. Here and there in this book I mention famous artists whose lives and work inspire me. Many of them have not concerned themselves with words like "perfection," but have painted to please their souls. I am especially intrigued by Anna Mary Robertson Moses. You probably know her as Grandma Moses. At the age of 78, she picked up a brush for the first time and started painting. She became incredibly famous for her nostalgic illustrations of an earlier, simpler time that lived vividly in her memory:

> *I look out the window sometimes to seek the color*
> *of the shadows and the different greens in the trees,*
> *but when I get ready to paint, I just close my eyes and imagine a scene.*

By its very nature, a garden is not about perfection. It is a living, changing being – just like you, just like me. I'm not the first person to say that a garden is a metaphor for life. My deepest desire in writing this book is that perhaps you, too, will consider and explore some of the gardening practices and ideals I have adopted over the years. I like to keep things simple and natural, organic and sustainable. One thing is certain: I am and have always been a self-proclaimed lazy, cheap gardener who loves to create balance, ease and beauty outdoors. I believe our gardens should be our love, not our labor of love.

I have tended and toiled in thousands of gardens as a professional and home gardener. I have seen a lot and solved a lot. I have also learned that I don't have to do everything myself. Knowing limitations and asking for help allows opportunities in and out of the garden. I am honored and excited to share with you my second-half-of-life way of thinking about gardens and gardening.

One more thing: I live and garden in Michigan. Your garden may be in California or Texas or Pennsylvania. The basic information in this book applies to gardeners everywhere. But when it comes to plant selection and tips for various climate conditions, I call on some of my wonderful expert gardening friends from other areas to give you the benefit of their wisdom.

Now, grab your favorite garden tools and kneepads and let's dig in together!

ONE

SIMPLICITY AND SUSTAINABILITY:
my liberating philosophy

⁂

*Simplicity is not an end in art. But we usually arrive
at simplicity as we approach the true sense of things.*

~ CONSTANTIN BRÂNCUȘI

I have never had a client, fellow gardener or friend ask me how to achieve a high maintenance garden. In fact, the one thing they know for sure is they want to keep it simple: low maintenance but beautiful.

I want to say right up front that there is no such thing as a maintenance-*free* garden or landscape. Gardens will always need a certain amount of attention – they're living things from Nature. But you can minimize maintenance and keep things simple – and still have a drop dead gorgeous garden. Of course you can.

Before I became a professional gardener I struggled in the garden (like many of us) with site selection, placement, choices, and all the other obstacles that often steal our joy and leave us feeling overwhelmed. The dynamics of my own gardens were constantly changing, like the weather.

Flowers in my garden

I was always rearranging, rethinking, renewing or removing. In hindsight, a lot of time, energy, effort and money poured into gardens that never quite suited me or my lifestyle. My gardens were pretty, but they were not a reflection of me. I knew it, but didn't know how to fix it.

If there was a philosophy of gardening – "The Rules" – I wasn't tuned into it. So, being someone who really *really* wanted to be a successful, not-frustrated gardener, I set out to look more deeply into my relationship with plants, with the seasons and the soil – and I discovered the profound wisdom that resides in a balanced ecosystem. A happy, healthy garden was a place where everything worked together in harmony, with the gardener being the facilitator and not the dictator. In time, I created my own foundation for gardening – call it my philosophy.

It is not about keeping up with others. It excludes memorizing botanical names and identifying every garden insect or noxious weed (that's what Google is for). Rather, it is an ongoing relationship, with deep and lasting experiences. For me, it is an opportunity to bring what I love to the garden; it makes me feel alive, rejuvenated and well. Gardens are my blank canvas, the one place to be fully expressed without limitation or prejudice. A garden is where hope is restored and relaxation is practiced.

Cultivating Sustainability

Sustainability is just about the most important thing to consider in planning and tending a garden. Thinking sustainably is an opportunity to enrich our lives and our souls through a better understanding of our plants and the many simple ways we can bring our garden into sync with Mother Nature. It's not a matter of giving anything up, but more about choosing a better way to achieve the same ends – and having a more heightened awareness of the rich inner life of your garden. And by "garden" I mean anything from acres of land to a tiny suburban back yard to a small container on a sunny deck.

Getting to this place of sustainability in the garden does not have to be tricky or "easier said than done." It does not mean you have to sacrifice beauty and design. But it does start with knowing in advance your desires, budget, physical capabilities, expected outcomes and commitments. And a few simple ground rules that will save you time, money, labor and heartbreak. Here is my Rule #1:

Right Plant, Right Place

You've probably heard the term. It is one of the fundamentals of sustainable (and successful) gardening. Let me tell you a cautionary tale about *not* choosing the right plant for the right place, and the unintended consequences that followed – both for my peace of mind and for the local landfill. I'm happy to say that my tale ends with an epiphany, but getting there was hard.

Many years ago I planted a very small 'Hakuronishiki' dappled willow in my landscape. And it GREW. It needed lots of attention to keep it in check. Clearly, it was not the right plant for the right place. A few years later, while hedging it (again), I realized that this just couldn't continue. But I was overwhelmed with guilt at the prospect of taking it out. Typically, I do not like removing a healthy tree unless it is not serving a garden or the gardener well. But on that particular day, I kept reminding myself that I had spent way too much time and energy trimming, pruning, bagging and tying up unwanted branches.

Hauling away the Hakuronishiki

My yard features plenty of plants, shrubs and trees that fit the space

My small, compact suburban yard is not the ideal space to grow large trees or shrubs. I had planted this tree back in the early days, before I knew better. As the tree grew and grew, so did my frustrations. The need to constantly hedge and prune it to "fit in" pushed me and my not-so-small overgrown tree over the edge. The work and waste created in one growing season was an ongoing concern; it was not a sustainable gardening practice. Nowhere near.

When I drove to the local waste and recycle management facility to dispose of the wilted willow piled in my trailer, I knew my decision was for the best. I had often visited the site – and still do – to dispose of yard waste for clients, and I've often pondered the enormity of the problem of the tons and tons of refuse that are poured into waste facilities every day – but this time, with this poor, rejected tree, it really got to me. I tried to imagine how much waste I've created in my lifetime. I knew I could do better.

I didn't tell this story to make us all feel guilty. It was really to show how we continue to grow and learn.

As gardeners, we have many opportunities during the planning and designing process to lessen the need to send garden waste to the landfill. One of the most fundamental practices is selecting the right plant for the right place. It is important to know the growth habits of plants before purchasing them. You don't want to end up with a 'Hakuronishiki' experience. The next time you go plant shopping, carefully read plant labels so constant pruning and hauling away waste will not consume your life and burden your local landfill.

A large part of sustainability is design. The wrong plant in the wrong place is one of the biggest mistakes we can make as gardeners. I had to learn to resist the urge to bring a plant into my garden simply because it looked gorgeous at the nursery. I had to give up ignoring or trying to manipulate the requirements for that plant to thrive, because it wasn't going to thrive.

I learned over and over again that it's not nice to fool Mother Nature. She always wins.

Strategies for Not Falling for the Wrong Plants at the Garden Center

Proper plant selection does not have to be a mystery or complicated if we do not get caught up in the beauty. It's important to stay connected to practicality and purpose. Plant purchases are significant investments in your homes, gardens and your life. Careful planning will allow you to reap what you sow – literally.

Below are things to think about *before* your next shopping trip and plant purchases. When you're at the nursery, dazzled by the array to choose from, you'll be glad you did your research beforehand.

Make sure you know your plant's growth potential before planting

> **Growth habit.** Plants for home gardeners are typically sold in two- three- five- and ten-gallon containers – even for large trees and shrubs that

will reach great heights and widths. You should not be confused or mislead by their enticing and attractive grow containers and petite size at the nursery. At the time of planting, position and install your new plantings based on its *mature growth potential*. The height and width at maturity (full grown) is on the plant label. It is very important to allow enough space for a plant to "fill in" – typically three years.

▶ **Plant characteristics.** If you are looking for year-round interest, winter interest, seasonal bloomers, textures, or all of the above, research a plant's characteristics to ensure you are getting what you want and serving your desired outcome.

▶ **Form.** The shape of a plant in its container is a good indicator of the shape the plant will be years later. Examine the entire plant – front, back, sides – to ensure it will look attractive from all angles when planted. Make sure you're showing off the plant's "good side."

▶ **Light requirement.** This is so important and not to be compromised. Know how much sunlight you get in different areas of the garden. Something to consider when estimating the number of sunny hours in areas you want to plant. The angle of the sun changes with the seasons and a sunny area in spring (high sun angle) may no longer be sunny in fall (low sun angle) when longer shadows are cast from nearby trees and buildings.

These Coreopsis love sunlight

  ▶ **Full sun:** six or more hours of direct sun per day

  ▶ **Partial sun or partial shade:** four to six hours of direct sun per day

  ▶ **Full shade:** less than four hours of direct sun per day

- **Heat and wind tolerance.** What does that mean? An example: a plant that is susceptible to high levels of heat should not be planted in a southern exposure against a potentially hot material structure unless it can, in fact, bear extreme temperatures. Remember, material like stone and brick hold heat and can impact a plant significantly. There are many plants that are heat and/or wind tolerant; in contrast, there are many that are not.

- **Drought tolerance.** If you garden in a drought-prone region, you need to know if plants can or cannot thrive there. Any good garden center in a drought-prone region should have a good selection of plants that will thrive there. But be aware that you could

Most Hostas are shade lovers, with a few exceptions – and they come in a variety of colors

also see lots of good looking plants that won't do well once you get them home. A little pre-shopping research will go a long way.

- **Soil preference.** Plants that thrive in sandy loam will struggle in heavy clay conditions, and vice-versa. So it's good to know your soil type and use soil amendments (or don't) accordingly. When in doubt about what kind of soil you have, you might make a small investment in a do-it-yourself soil test kit, which will let you know the basic components and pH of your soil.

Plant shopping and trips to the garden center should never be overwhelming. If you do your homework first, the rewards are plentiful! Just don't forget your shopping list!

Designing and planning gardens while shopping can be as dangerous (and as tempting) as food shopping with hunger pangs. Both should be avoided!

Instant Gratification: sometimes necessary but not always recommended

Evergreens provide privacy, but need time for growth

Sofia was a new client. She and her husband wanted immediate screening (privacy) in their backyard and did not want to wait one second longer. Aside from installing a privacy fence, a mass planting of evergreens was the most practical option for year-round coverage. I explained to the couple that over time the appropriately selected number of plants based on the design would fill in nicely, providing the privacy they wanted. But the operative words were "over time," and the couple planned to reside at the home for less than

five years. They didn't want to wait for their privacy, so their preference was to plant as many evergreens as possible in the space, for immediate gratification and coverage. Yes, the evergreens will quickly achieve a lush look; they will also eventually become overgrown for the space. I will address the difference between lush and overgrown on page 52, and the consequences of overgrown gardens.

I understand the temptation and have experienced the same eagerness for immediate gratification many times myself. But the most satisfying and fulfilling part of second-half-of-life gardening is building into it the anticipation of what's coming next. The beauty and reality Mother Nature delivers requires no hurrying, pushing or prodding. Waiting is a lovely way to capture and appreciate what is truly happening in a garden – patiently allowing for a plant to reach its maturity and potential in its own time. It's a gardener's reward for a job well done.

Three Sustainable Practices for a Garden in Sync with Nature

Here is a starter list of sustainable practices to make life simpler in the garden. I'll dig deeper with you as we go along.

1. Reduce weeds by creating heavily planted garden beds. If you walk your gardens, you will notice weeds are usually prolific where plants are not growing. Amazingly, very few weeds grow under a plant. Don't be shy – fill up your garden beds with the right plant in the right place. You'll be pleased with the end result and how much time you have to spare! Concerned about overcrowding? Don't be. There's such a thing as "crowded but lush" (if that sounds like an oxymoron, I'll show you what I mean on page 52).

2. **Make the most of your water.** We all know that water is a precious resource and getting more precious every day. A few ways to hold onto that water:

~ Concaved or flat garden beds. They soak up water very well, but steep garden beds do not. Here's an example: *Berms* (raised garden beds) allow you to control the soil and drainage of a new garden bed, which is good. Steep berms (as seen here), however, are not good because water runs off and encourages erosion. Steep berms can be risky business because plants will not absorb the water

necessary to develop healthy root systems. An ideal practice when building a berm is to flatten out the top so water can drain down through the soil and not run off. It is also a good practice to create a "mulch well" around newly planted trees and shrubs. The mulch well holds in the water, allowing it to drain down through the root system where it is needed.

~ Less lawn, more garden! Did you know lawns require far more resources than a well-designed, well-planted garden? I'll have lots to say about lawns and lawn alternatives. I found this information from the EPA very surprising: "residential outdoor water use across the United States accounts for nearly nine billion gallons of water each day,

mainly for landscape irrigation. The average U.S. household uses more water outdoors than most American homes use for showering and washing clothes combined." Once a garden is established, it does not require constant watering, like lawns do – just saying!

~ Water harvesting. This is an excellent way to reduce water usage and costly water bills during the growing season. Water harvesting can have a major impact on the environment and is extremely beneficial to our natural waterways. The ultimate goal of water harvesting is to retain rainwater on your property and out of city storm drains. In the chapters that follow, I will share easy ways to harvest water, like the rainwater barrel above – every drop counts!

3. **Replicate a natural forest ecosystem in your garden space.** Nature is the expert; we should take more cues from her. We gardeners have the best of intentions, but sometimes less is more. Can you image blowing or raking leaves in the forest? I doubt that ever happens. On page 18, I share why I "leave the leaves," and the benefits they provide to us, the ecosystem and wildlife.

A Sustainable Garden and Wildlife

One day I was relaxing in a favorite chair in my gardens enjoying the peaceful sound of flowing water in a nearby fountain. Out of nowhere, a sweet little black squirrel hopped onto the fountain and began drinking from it. He did not know I was there; I sat perfectly still so I would not startle him. And then he scurried off, belly full of water, thirst quenched as I watched with sheer joy and deep gratitude. In that moment, the squirrel unknowingly improved my life and wellbeing, and I hope I improved his, too, by providing him a place to rest and find water.

Simple moments like this remind me why I love and appreciate gardening. In fact, I enjoy the wildlife who visit my gardens as much as I do gardening. I believe that in order to have balance and harmony in the garden, we must be more accepting of what nature provides. It may sound cliché, but my second-half-of-life gardening philosophy is that there's enough for everyone and everything. It's about cultivating a generous spirit and working with nature, not against her. My gardens would have far less life and meaning without something flying, sitting, resting, drinking, eating or digging in it besides myself. And I include the squirrels, rabbits and other furred

Squirrels are a part of backyard nature

and feathered beings that I share my little piece of earth with.

I do not use, endorse or believe in poisonous or inhumane wildlife controls in the garden.

A word about pesticides and herbicides: My theory is that any product that recommends you "suit up" to apply it and posts a sign to keep pregnant women, children and pets off for 24 hours can't be good. Besides, wildlife can't read. They don't know to stay away. Herbicides used on lawns (weed killers) take a terrible toll on wildlife. More than seven million wild birds are estimated to die annually in the U.S. due to the use of lawn chemicals.

Sprinkle garlic powder on mature plants to deter rabbits

I know how frustrating it is to plant lovely spring bulbs, then watch the squirrels dig them up. So how do I rectify their sometimes-damaging (but necessary for survival) behavior? For the most part, I have surrendered. After years of planting spring bulbs, I no longer wait for an arrival that never happens. Thank you, squirrels. I don't plant spring bulbs anymore; instead, I admire the beautiful displays others have planted. Now, I just throw a handful of nuts to the squirrels and enjoy watching them come close in growing trust. It's easier that way.

When planting my vegetable gardens, I plant some for me and some for the wildlife. Each season I attempt to harvest strawberries but unfortunately (or fortunately) the wildlife beat me to my best crops. I have simply reconciled myself to their presence in my garden and understand that they belong there, too. Now, I head to the local farmers market, content that I can support the farmers and the wildlife. Most of all, I am flattered that these pesky but very entertaining critters like my choice of crops and that I am able to provide for them, too. If that sounds like a capitulation, maybe it is. But it's an arrangement the critters, the garden and I can live with.

Plant what you love. If something eats it, be content knowing you contributed to their well-being. If they don't eat one thing, they'll find something else to munch on. Their playful antics or majestic beauty and presence are well worth it. As you know, a gardener's work is never done. We (me and you) have been chosen to care for the earth, nature, and wildlife. It is our gift, it is our responsibility.

Our task must be to free ourselves...
by widening our circle of compassion to embrace
all living creatures and the whole of nature in its beauty.

~ ALBERT EINSTEIN

Attracting beneficial wildlife is so easy: simply plant a garden. It does not have to be large. Even one small container filled with their favorites becomes an excellent food source and habitat for birds, bees, butterflies and other pollinators. An online search will bring up lots of plant lists for various pollinator friends in different regions.

Some things you can do to welcome wildlife:

▶ **Give 'em a place to call home.** Worms, beetles and all kinds of insects will quickly take up residence in compost piles, and bins and rotting logs provide a natural habitat and food source. It's a good thing. Don't forget toads and frogs – nature's champion insecticides! Toads eat many kinds of insects including snails, slugs, and beetles. One toad is capable of eating up to 1000 insects a day. Lay out a few rocks for these welcome garden guests. Turn a broken ceramic or terracotta pot over and use as a toad house. Let's roll out the red carpet for these little guys!

▶ **Quench their thirst.** Water is critical for the survival of all wildlife. Most wildlife die in winter due to lack of water, not food. A small birdbath, free-standing fountain or lovely pond is a wonderful way to attract a variety of wildlife. Keep water levels in birdbaths low (less than an inch); birds can't swim.

▶ **Give 'em shelter.** Hedges, deciduous shrubs and evergreens provide food and shelter from predators and protect wildlife from harsh cold winters.

"Dear pollinators: You're invited to a garden party!"

Plant pollination and the production of crops are highly dependent on the critical function of bees and butterflies. Environment America, a citizen-funded, state-based environmental advocacy organization, says, "Millions of bees are dying off, with alarming consequences for our environment and our food supply. We rely on bees to pollinate everything from almonds to strawberries to the hay used to feed dairy cows. What happens if the bees disappear? It's simple: no bees, no food."

Plant a Plant for the Bees:

Alyssum	Anise Hyssop	Bee Balm
Borage	Catmint	Coneflower
Cosmos	Dill	Goldenrod
Hollyhock	Lavender	Parsley
Poppy	Rosemary	Sage
Salvia	Sunflower	Thyme
Verbena	Yarrow	Zinnia

The continued existence of butterflies is critical, too. These gorgeous creatures are cherished visitors in the garden. American poet Robert Frost eloquently describes butterflies as "flowers that fly and all but sing." One of the most recognizable of our butterflies is the majestic Monarch, and we've all heard the disturbing stories of their habitat loss as they make their incredible journey of migration. The good thing is that gardeners everywhere are responding by creating butterfly habitat stations for these long-distance beauties.

Did you know? Adult butterflies are attracted to red, yellow, orange, pink and purple blossoms that are flat-topped or clustered and have short flower tubes.

Attracting Monarch Butterflies to Your Garden

Here are four things you can do to attract Monarchs to your gardens, from my friend Kylee Baumle. She is a devoted advocate for Monarchs. Her latest book is *The Monarch: Saving Our Most-Loved Butterfly*.

▷ **Milkweed.** Since milkweed (*Asclepias* spp.) plants are essential for a Monarch to raise their young, growing it increases your chances of attracting Monarchs to your garden. There are perennial varieties as well as annual ones and these can be grown in containers or in the ground. Consult with a local garden center to see which varieties grow best in your area.

▷ **Milkweed variety.** Provide more than one kind of milkweed if you want Monarchs to lay eggs in your garden and not just visit it. Like people, Monarchs seem to have preferences for their "flavor" of milkweed. Some prefer swamp milkweed (*Asclepias incarnata*), while others flock to common milkweed (*A. syriaca*). By growing two or three different types, you'll increase your chances of having Monarchs frequent your garden.

- **Host plants for nectar.** Monarch butterflies also need host plants to provide nectar for nourishment and energy, especially if they're migrating. A few of their favorites are zinnias, goldenrod, coreopsis, black-eyed Susans, coneflowers, asters, blazing star (*Liatris* spp.), and bee balm (*Monarda* spp.)

- **Water.** As Monarchs go about their day, they need water as well as food. Though nectar provides some, they will also seek out other water sources. You can provide this as easily as setting out a plate with water on it. The plate works best, rather than a bowl, because the water will be shallow and the dry edges of the plate provide a safe resting place for the Monarch to sit and sip.

Want to invite butterflies to your garden? Plant some zinnias, coneflowers, asters and more

A warning about pesticides: This seems intuitive, but be sure you aren't sabotaging your efforts at attracting Monarchs (and other pollinators) to your garden by using pesticides. These can include fungal treatments as well as soil drenches, which can become incorporated into the actual plant. Spraying for mosquitoes will kill mosquitoes, but it can also kill butterflies and other beneficial insects. And just because something is organic doesn't mean it's harmless to Monarchs, so use with discretion.

Leave the Leaves

One day when I was playing in my garden, I bent down and picked up a handful of soil. It was a rich, black color and felt like gold in my hands; I knew it had everything to do with years of decayed fallen leaves. Hence its nickname: black gold.

The garden practice of leaving the leaves is exactly how it sounds. Literally, leave the leaves. Did you know leaving the leaves is one of the most beneficial, economical and easiest garden practices you'll ever do? I stopped raking my fallen leaves years ago and I am glad I did. I'm sure the neighborhood thought I was crazy or neglecting a necessary city seasonal chore, but today I have the healthiest soil in town and you can, too!

Fallen leaves play a vital role in our ecosystem, they provide:

- Food and shelter for wildlife
- A place for bugs to overwinter
- Nutrients to the soil
- Fertilizer for soil
- A natural weed suppressant
- Protection for roots in winter

Want another reason to leave the leaves? The U.S. Environmental Protection Agency says: "[L]eaves and other yard debris account for more than 13 percent of the nation's solid waste – a whopping 33 million tons a year." Need one more reason to leave the leaves? National Wildlife Federation naturalist David Mizejewski says, "The less time you spend raking leaves, the more

time you'll have to enjoy the gorgeous fall weather and the wildlife that visits your garden."

The simple practice of "leave the leaves" contributes significantly to the reduction of waste in landfills, and the health and wellbeing of our wildlife and ecosystem.

Warning: turning in your rake and breaking the habit may be easier said than done. But after a season of no raking, you and Mother Nature will be glad you did!

TWO

GARDENING WITH COMFORT AND EASE
taking care of you

There can be no other occupation like gardening in which,
if you were to creep up behind someone at their work,
you would find them smiling.

~ MIRABEL OSLER

I love playing in the soil and getting dirty. Gone are the days of glamorous, well-manicured fingernails (and toenails) – the tradeoff is minuscule in comparison. Not only do I love the rewards of a beautiful garden, I love the idea of being active.

Gardening is a practical and beneficial way to stay healthy physically and mentally. In fact, research has found that the "friendly" *Mycobacterium vaccae* bacteria found in soil may affect the brain like anti-depressant drugs. Apparently the bacterium stimulates the portion of the brain that produces serotonin. Perhaps that explains the reasons for the strong sense of calmness and satisfaction we feel while gardening. I am not surprised.

The three most important components in continuing our passion to garden in the second half of life:

- **Staying healthy**
- **Using proper tools**
- **Dressing comfortably**

Tip: Do your chores that require standing first, then hit the ground. I think getting up and down constantly adds undo stress to the body. When I am kneeling on the ground, I like to stay there until I am finished.

Staying Healthy: Garden Yoga

You may know the saying: *If I woke up in the morning and nothing hurt, I would think I was dead.* We gardeners can certainly attest to that. To alleviate sore muscles, I highly recommend stretching before and after gardening. One way I remain flexible and resilient is practicing yoga while gardening. I stretch my body before, during and after to avoid injury, gain strength, and continue doing what I love. If you already practice yoga, you'll recognize my three favorite and very simple poses: Forward Fold, Cat-Cow and Squat. If you're new to yoga, check out these poses online. You'll find lots of illustrations and videos.

Listening to my body while gardening and knowing when to start and stop is important to staying healthy. Yoga also helps build strength, endurance, balance and flexibility, and it's easy to practice while gardening. *Namaste!*

Did you know? The development of yoga can be traced back to over 5,000 years ago, but some researchers think that yoga may be up to 10,000 years old. The earliest writings on yoga were transcribed on fragile palm leaves that were easily damaged, destroyed or lost. (Yoga.com)

Tools to Make Things Easier

A gardener's work can be so much easier using proper tools. And you don't have to spend a lot of money. In fact, I purchased two favorite garden tools at a local flea market several years ago for less than ten dollars. Through the years, my bargain-find steel leaf rake and pitchfork have lasted longer than the more expensive ones I have purchased. Plus, they are lighter in weight, another important factor to keep in mind when selecting tools.

It is important to have tools that feel comfortable in your hands and are easy to maneuver.

My favorite garden tools:

▶ **Bypass pruner** is an essential garden tool. Like Goldilocks, a pruner has to be just right – not too big, not too small. A pruner must be a perfect fit in your hands for comfort and safety. I clipped the tip of my finger (stitches necessary) using a pruner that was way too big and cumbersome.

My mini D-handle shovel is the best tool for digging holes for plants.

- **Pruner pouch** is a must! Without my pouch, I would leave my pruner everywhere. It's a great way to store your pruner when you are not using it and it protects your clothes while carry it. *Bonus:* I always know where to find my pruner – on my right side for easy access.
- **Household scissors** are handy and perfect for cutting and trimming when a pruner is not necessary.
- **Lopper** is a must have to cut branches that are too large for your bypass pruner. I like the ones that extend to reach things higher up.
- **Half-moon spade** is the ideal tool for edging garden beds and removing/scoring sod.
- **Tine steel leaf rake** is preferred over a plastic rake. This rake has flexibility when using, it feels less resistant in the pull than a plastic one. I use this rake to spread mulch; flip it over and use the backside for an even, finished look in the garden. It's like icing a cake!
- **Hard tine rake** is perfect for evenly spreading soil.

- **Mini D-handle shovel** is my favorite digging tool! This pint-size shovel is perfect for planting. Sometimes standing and digging can be hard on your back. I love getting on my knees and digging with this little gem. Try it, you'll like it!
- **Pitch fork** is perfect for scooping mulch. My vintage pitchfork is much lighter than the ones you buy today. Search flea markets and garage sales. Mine was quite the bargain; it cost $2.00 and I have been using it for years.
- **Five-in-one** is a painter's tool but I have renamed it to a seven-in-one! This small, inexpensive tool is perfect for removing weeds from cracks. Flip it over and use the flat edge to remove moss from hard surfaces. It's the best investment ever.
- **Wheelbarrow** is necessary to lug all these tools and much more around the garden!

Tip: Spray-painting the handles of garden tools a bright color makes them much easier to find if you have buried them in a heap of debris or dumped them in your compost bin.

Work Wear: Comfy, Practical Clothes

I'm all about comfort and practicality. My personal choice for gardening clothes is long pants with a forgiving waist. I want my legs protected from nicks and bruises. I like to keep the sun off my face, so I wear a baseball cap. It doesn't get in the way like big, flouncy garden hats. I don't spend a lot of money on gloves because I wear them out so quickly. I try to protect my arms as much as possible from the elements, but sometimes it's too hot for long sleeves. By the way: I am still waiting for someone to sew a gardening shirt with a built in bra (a huge obstacle).

I have a problem with shoes because the toes wear out faster than the heels from crawling around on the ground. I like

Wearing a hat is a must outside.

wearing shoes that are light so it does not feel like I am carrying weights on my feet. Let me rave about Wellies for a moment: waterproof and comfortable is a must. Rubber boots are ideal when it's raining or when walking through your garden after it rains. Plus, there are so many fun colors and patterns!

Sometimes working in a light rain on a warm day feels great. I slip on my raingear and relish working in conjunction with Mother Nature. There's something very soothing and magical about working in the rain.

▶ One last thing: **knee pads**. Protecting the cartilage and tissue of your knees is extremely important. There are many comfortable styles to choose from. Some garden pants have inserts to slip the pads in, which are very useful while gardening.

Outdoor essentials like gloves, kneepads and pruner pouch make gardening easier

I aspire to comfort and ease in the garden and in my life. I often find inspiration in the life and work of famous artists. Henri Matisse is an artist I admire for his colorful, fun and creative portrait and landscape paintings. If you are not familiar with his work, I encourage you to research him – his work is delightful. I find comfort and ease in his paint strokes; each feels effortless.

One thing I find inspirational and profound about Matisse is his will to continue his work despite physical limitations; like us, we want to continue our work in the garden. At the age of 80, Matisse reinvented himself when he could no longer stand to use his paintbrush. Despite his ailing health, Matisse continued working and produced a new technique of "carving into color'" by creating paper cutouts in bold colors. Matisse believed work cured everything; one has to admire his determination to continue doing what he loved. Matisse died in 1954; he was 84.

Sometimes I feel society gives up on second-half-of-lifers way too soon when, in fact, we have so much wisdom and experience to offer. Like Matisse, we all have the will and desire to continue our work and make a difference, whether we are in the garden or not.

What I dream of is an art of balance,
of purity and serenity devoid of troubling or depressing subject matter
– a soothing, calming influence on the mind,
rather like a good armchair which provides relaxation from physical fatigue.

~ HENRI MATISSE

THREE

WHERE DOES YOUR GARDEN GROW?
plant hardiness zones and microclimates

❦

Climate is what we expect. Weather is what we get.
~ MARK TWAIN

In my online community I like to share plants and their characteristics for others to enjoy. Based on my readers' responses, there is often some confusion about whether or not a plant will grow where they live. So, before going any further, I want to demystify a perplexing yet very important topic: ZONES.

Knowing your hardiness zone first, and then a plant's, will help you select plants that will thrive in your location. The first thing I look for when reading a plant label is its hardiness zone. If a plant is not favorable to my zone and it wouldn't perform well for its intended purpose in the garden, I move on.

For the record, there are eleven plant hardiness zones in the U.S. and southern Canada, based on minimum winter temperatures (the higher your zone number the warmer your winter temperatures). You can find your hardiness zone by visiting The United States Department of Agriculture's website at: http://www.planthardiness.ars.usda.gov. Each zone number represents a 10-degree increase or decrease of winter temperatures from the adjacent zone. Note: sometimes a zone will end in "b," like my own zone 5b. This indicates a 5-degree sub-zone within zone 5. I wouldn't blame you if you were scratching your head now.

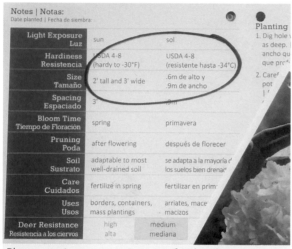

Plant tags give zone requirements for the plant

How do you go about evaluating a plant for your zone? In this case, it's "right plant, right zone."

Using my southeast Michigan garden as an example: My hardiness zone is 5b (winter temps down to -10 to -15°F), but northern Michigan is zone 4 – lower winter temperatures). When I shop for perennials and evergreens, I select plants that are hardy to my 5b zone: they will tolerate temperatures that get down to -15°F.

Note: Perennials with higher hardiness zones (example: 7-11) may be considered annuals in colder climates like zones 4, 5, or 6.

A plant label will read like this: *"hardiness zones 5-9."* With that information, I know the plant will *likely* grow and thrive in my zone. In contrast, I would not purchase a perennial or evergreen if the label read *"hardiness zone 11"* because it is not hardy to my zone and will not survive Michigan's cold winters. But I *would* select and purchase a plant whose hardiness zone is 11 as a summer annual, because it will grow and thrive in my zone in the warm months and be finished by the time winter comes.

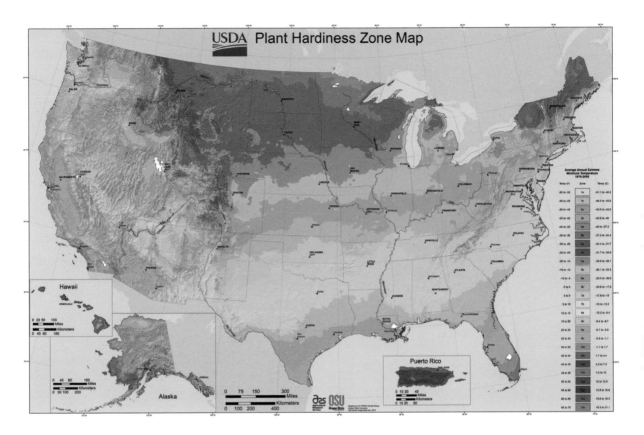

USDA Plant Hardiness Zone Map

Microclimate mysteries. Now, there's a big "but" and it's an important one when it comes to hardiness zones. Have you ever had a neighbor admire a plant in your garden and declare she could not grow the identical plant in hers? Here's why: You and your neighbor may have different microclimates in your gardens. These can even vary significantly from one garden bed to the next: a planting bed under a large shade tree can have a different microclimate from a bed twenty feet away in full sun. The cooler north side of your house has a different microclimate from the warmer south side.

This sounds crazy, doesn't it? However, careful consideration of microclimates can make all the difference in the world for plants. Even small variations in sun, shade, soil, wind, water, salt and elevation may contribute to different planting scenarios from one area to another. For instance, my friend grows the most gorgeous Bee Balm in her garden; in mine, they just don't thrive and I am not exactly sure why. I confess I have a bad case of plant envy but I have resigned myself to enjoying hers from afar. I chalk it up the variables of microclimate.

Do you love Hydrangeas, but...?

I get many client requests to plant gorgeous Mophead *(Macrophylla)* hydrangea varieties like 'Endless Summer', 'Forever Pink', 'Penny Mac' and 'Nikko Blue', just to name a few. However, I have yet to see one that has performed well (had reliable blooms each season) in anyone's garden in my 5b zone, so I don't plant them. Instead, I plant *Paniculata* varieties of Hydrangea such as 'Little

Paniculata Hydrangea give off masses of blooms

Lime', 'Little Lamb', 'Pinky Winky' and many others. Hydrangeas are gifts that keep on giving in the garden, but be sure to plant species that won't disappoint you.

If a plant does not perform well in your garden when you have followed all the rules, remember how hardiness zones and microclimates can sometimes change the rules. It's not you, it's Mother Nature.

Funny as this might sound, I think we have hardiness zones too – personal ones, zones we thrive in and those we don't. For me, I can spend every day on my hands and knees weeding gardens, no problem. But please don't ask me to send out greeting cards or contribute to a bake sale; I will surely disappoint you and myself. I think we are a lot like plants; it's important for us to know where we thrive at this point in life.

FOUR

GARDEN STYLING
finding balance, ease and beauty

⁂

To order space is to give it meaning.

~ ISAMU NOGUCHI

A sustainable garden begins with a design that is functional, cost efficient, visually attractive, environmentally friendly and easy to maintain. Let's see how to achieve a design that incorporates these criteria. My design principles and practices are applicable for any hardiness zone. I am going to keep this simple with some basic garden terms and design concepts. If you're relatively new to gardening, it will be good to know…if you're an old hand in the garden, it's here if you'd like a review.

When I visit a public garden or look through one of the luscious garden magazines, like *Fine Gardening* or *Garden Design*, I find myself having an emotional reaction to some of the gardens and not so much to others, even though the photos are equally lovely. Why is that? I'm responding on a subconscious level to the "vibe" – something about the design that draws me to it and rocks my boat.

6 Basic Design Tips

Plant selecting and shopping can be challenging without a game plan. I believe a well-thought garden sketch or design is extremely helpful and beneficial. It's your roadmap that will take second guessing out of plant material selections and placements. My advice: before you head to your favorite garden center, remember these easy-to-achieve garden design tips:

- **Odd number plantings.** Odd number plantings make a strong visual statement and impact. The eye gravitates to plants and other objects that are presented in odd numbers – like 1, 3 and 5.

- **Year-round interest.** This Michigander needs to see interest in the garden year-round. So don't forget about winter. Research plants specific to your hardiness zone that will provide winter interest too, such as evergreens, peeling bark and ornamental grasses.

- **Elements other than plants,** like boulders, bird baths, garden art, water features, metal structures, or outdoor benches make a strong visual four-season impact, too.

- **Obvious entrance.** Create a front entrance that is welcoming and visible from the street. Concealed or hidden entrances can be uninviting and may have the potential to create a hazard or security issue. New guests should never wonder where your front door is!

- **Inside looking out.** Sit in a favorite chair or couch with an outside view or stand at your kitchen window. Your garden should be enjoyed from inside *and* outside!

▶ **Color, texture, interest and contrast** are key to bringing a garden alive with energy. For instance, consider planting a spiky ornamental grass like 'Karl Foerster' Reed Grass next to a big, flouncy, blooming Hydrangea shrub. Or, pair a dark leaf perennial like 'Midnight Lady' Ligularia with the ever-so-bold 'Lime Ricky' Coral Bell (this is a fantastic pairing for a shade garden). Be daring and creative; it's your garden – plant what you love (in the right place)!

Inviting Entries

How do you create an inviting entry into your garden? Some words of advice from garden expert P. Allen Smith: "Punctuating an entry serves the practical purpose of guiding guests through the garden. If you want visitors to stop for a moment at an entrance, place a fragrant plant nearby. A pot of fragrant flowers or herbs near a gate, door or at the bend in a path will encourage people to pause and enjoy the garden."

Plant profiling: what you need to know

When designing and selecting plants, it's important to know how a plant performs: who's here to stay and who isn't. Do you want a single-season plant or one that will be with you year after year? Do you want a plant that loses its leaves in winter or keeps them year round? Sometimes horticultural lingo can be confusing, especially if you are a new gardener. To know the answers to the questions above, you should have a basic understanding of the three most commonly used words in the garden world: **annual, perennial** and **evergreen**.

▶ **Annual:** An annual is short-lived. It completes its life cycle in a single growing season and then dies. For summer annuals in colder areas, you want to wait to plant until after the last spring frost; with the first winter frost the plant will be finished. Winter annuals will germinate in autumn, maturing the following spring or summer. In warmer areas, the growing seasons will be extended, depending on the arrival of frost. Examples: Petunias, Lantana, Sweet Pea, Ageratum, Bachelor's Button, Cosmos, Zinnia.

Petunias are a popular annual

Lantana flowers typically change color as they mature

- **Perennial:** A perennial lives for more than one or two years. Depending on where you live (colder climates), it may die back in winter, but reappear in spring. Others will stay looking beautiful all year. Many perennials can be divided, so you can easily "make babies" and save lots of money. Examples: Dahlia, Coneflower, Gaura, Coral Bell, Daisy.

- **Evergreen:** An evergreen is a plant that keeps its foliage through the year. It does lose some leaves or needles at times, but never all at once, whether it's a shrub or a tree. (This contrasts with deciduous plants, which drop their foliage at the end of the growing season – but first, many of them put on a spectacular display of color). I remember when the true meaning of evergreen finally sank in for me: ever green, green forever, as in green year-round in the garden! I love those aha moments. Examples: Arborvitae, Juniper, Boxwood, Spruce, Hemlock. See page 80 for more amazing evergreens.

Note: Perennials with higher hardiness zones (example: 7-11) may be considered annuals in colder climates like zones 4, 5, or 6.

These dahlias pack gorgeous color

Juniper foliage stays green year-round

Balance, Ease and Beauty

For me, good design in the garden means embracing balance, ease and beauty in the design process. Let me explain how that works:

- **Balance** is an understanding of limitations, lifestyle, space, climate, hardiness zone and available resources. It is the framework for enjoyment and success. Yes, breakdowns happen in the garden, but why add unnecessary angst? Instead, work with what you have and within your abilities and limitations.

- **Ease** eliminates or reduces inputs such as water, pesticides and fertilizers. Ease is the link to less work and memorable moments while serving nature, the environment and ourselves.

- **Beauty** is what excites and drives us all to gardening. Beauty in the garden is a work of art – your art, your impression. It will keep you coming back for more; it's your icing on the cake!

An out-of-balance scenario

Now, let's look at another example of what can happen when you have the wrong plant in the wrong place, and how it disrupts the sense of ease, for you and the environment:

Three large ornamental shrubs with the growth potential of 12 feet are planted in front of a large picture window. The bottom of the large picture window measures four feet from the ground. Selecting 12-foot shrubs for that spot is not considered a sustainable practice because:

▶ **The shrubs will require ongoing pruning and hedging** to maintain an acceptable height. If the shrubs are not maintained, they will eventually block the outside view from the inside and cover the large picture window from the outside. Neither is ideal.

▶ **Unwanted waste** generated from unnecessary maintenance defies sustainability. The goal is to keep waste out of landfills and to recycle when you can.

Let's imagine a different scenario using the same large picture window. A shrub with a mature height of 4-5 feet is a much better choice. A right plant in the right place will never get too big and will not need constant pruning or hedging to maintain an ideal height. I especially love when flowering ornamental shrubs like Incrediball Hydrangea or Double Knockout Rose peep up over a window casing – a delightful display indoors!

▶ **The maintenance alley.** Always, always, always take out your measuring tape when planting. If you are planting an ornamental shrub near your home whose mature width is 10 feet, allow at least two feet between your home and the shrub at its maximum width. Leave enough elbow room to maneuver around between your home and your landscape for maintenance like painting or washing windows. This space is called the "maintenance alley."

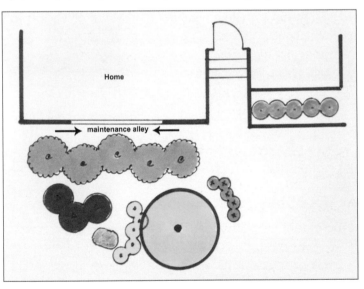

My Room with a View

Built during the 1950s, the homes in my neighborhood are nestled very close to one another. In fact, they are so close that when I look out my dining room window, I can see my neighbors' vehicles in their driveways. I love my neighbors, don't get me wrong. But in this stage of life, a room with a view matters. So, I planted a hedge of lovely 'Invincibelle® Spirit' Hydrangea *(Hydrangea arborescens)* outside my window. Now when I am sitting in my dining room or passing through from another room, big pink beautiful blooms offer a wonderful surprise. I never tire of the large blossoms gracefully billowing in the wind. A subtle change, like a hedge of Hydrangea, can sometimes have the biggest impact. Treat yourself to a room with a view!

Color

When we think about gardens, we think of color. Color makes us happy; it joyfully lifts us up. Since we have a deliriously wide palette to choose from, we paint our gardens with color, and lots of it. And I'm not just talking about flowering plants. The range of colors and texture in plant foliage is endless. In my garden designs, I like to look past the more temporary seasonal color provided by annual flowers and find ways to juxtapose interesting foliage tones.

But here's another way to think about color in a garden that you may not have considered: When designing your gardens, do not dismiss the use of a monochromic theme.

A "Moon Garden"

One day, I was visiting a client for the first time. We were scheduled to meet in her back gardens. As I walked briskly around her home to the yard, I stopped dead in my tracks. Before my eyes were the most gorgeous, lush green-and-white formal gardens I had ever seen. Commonly known as a "moon garden," an all-white garden may be seen as lacking, but monochromic gardens like this one leave a lasting impression and create a warm appreciation for nature. Each time I tend monochromatic gardens, my admiration for their simplicity, elegance and grace is renewed.

These white peonies are perfect in a "moon garden"

Forgoing a wide range of various colors may be a compromise for some gardeners. But, if you are thinking about creating a new garden, consider selecting and combining plants of similar hues. They needn't be white tones, like the moon garden I visited. Colors like dark purple, violet, and lavender or pastel pink, hot pink and dark rose can be lovely monochromatic combinations. I think you will be pleasantly surprised at the harmonious balance and outcome they provide. Still not convinced? Next time you are at a garden center, gather up some plants of similar hues and group them together. Then step back and take a look at what can happen with a closely connected palette.

A Color Tip: Sometimes gardens with too much color appear busy and chaotic; they don't allow the eye to rest. Color brings balance and flow to the garden, so consider your color palette during the design process, too.

Spring bulbs add wonderful color in the garden. They are a simple and delightful way to greet the growing season after a long winter. Check bloom times. With a little planning, you can enjoy colorful flowers from early to late spring!

A Garden is More Than Plants Alone

Artful Finds

What are artful finds and why are they important in the garden? A garden will always be a work-in-progress. It is a living thing, a partner in your life's story. The late poet, painter and gardener Robert Dash called gardens "a form of autobiography" and I believe it. We travel, we have triumphs and tragedies, we grow. And we have an instinct to mark memorable moments by adding things – objects – to our gardens. Incorporating artful finds, objects other than plants, creates unexpected interest and wonder…and often a visual connection to someone or something in our lives.

Garden art is a way to bring more color and texture to a landscape. A garden bench invites a visitor to stop for a moment and let the world go quiet. A lovely fountain brings hummingbirds and butterflies; a statue brings whimsy or formality. Every artful find is an expression of the gardener's personal taste and style. There are countless ways to incorporate different mediums into the garden. Go ahead and let your personality shine through, says P. Allen Smith, gardener extraordinaire. Make your garden a one-of-a-kind, your kind!

I especially love recycled art in gardens. Recycled, upcycled, and reused materials keep things out of landfills and are an excellent sustainable practice. When the opportunity arises, I advise clients to search their homes before buying something new; chances are they already have what they need – there's no need to buy more. Besides, giving life back to something old and forgotten is the best feeling ever!

A note from my heart: Sometimes the best artful find is the one you bring back with you from a nature walk. May you venture into nature in search of more unconventional artful finds – those that cannot be purchased, only discovered.

Rock Your Gardens

These large boulders serve as a beautiful retaining wall for the yard and garden

Rocks provide unique accents and excellent focal points in the garden as they are natural yet unexpected. Their hard surfaces complement garden spaces effortlessly, enhancing many different designs and styles. For instance: a variety of rocks laid out in gentle flowing curves will create a natural and functional dry creek bed. You can also group rocks together, like mass plantings, or use as a single specimen, like an ornament tree. Large boulders serve as additional seating in the garden. Place one in the garden by your entrance or under a tree – wherever a resting place is needed. It's also fun to border a garden bed with small rocks for an attractive and natural bed line. And, as an added bonus, they are 100% maintenance-free.

Here are a few tips about choosing and adding rocks and boulders to your beds:

- **Boulders and rocks are very heavy** and will more than likely need to be delivered and placed by a professional. If they are rocks and boulders that are already native to your property, you'll likely need help with placement.

- **Consider the scale of your home and gardens when selecting.** A small rock, 1' x 1', placed in a very large space will appear underwhelming. Conversely, a large boulder, 3' x 3', in a very small space will appear too large. Right stone, right place.

- **Take time to pick the most attractive side** of your boulder before it is permanently placed since it is difficult to move a boulder or large rock once it has been placed.
- **Think about plants.** Plants and rocks balance each other nicely in the garden. Boulders in the garden offer excellent planting opportunities, so be sure to plant around the boulder.
- **Planting in odd numbers applies to boulders, too.** When possible, think one, three, five, etc. – depending on the size of your space. Using odd numbers,

A well-placed boulder is an attractive addition to any garden

you will allow the boulders to make an even grander statement in your garden.

One of my favorite American artists is Isamu Noguchi (1904-1988), revered as an artist's artist for his abstract sculptures and public garden designs. His work in stone and wood and public spaces is the epitome of simplicity, yet profound and unforgettable. He deeply understood the garden as a space that gives nourishment to the spirit.

In many ways gardeners are artists, too. Through our hard work and dedication, we develop a better understanding and relationship with nature, and in doing so we give meaning to our gardens. "I am always learning, always discovering," Noguchi wrote. That could be said of anyone who gardens…at any age.

FIVE

SMALL GARDEN ABUNDANCE
making the most of the space you have

❧

Do the best that you can in the space where you are, and be kind.
~ SCOTT NEARING

I live in a suburb with a tiny front and back yard. Some might assume that my gardening opportunities would be limited. I am here to say that is a myth. I have utilized every inch of available space with plants I love, and you can too!

You don't have to feel limited as a gardener. Big things grow in small spaces! In fact, the older I get, the more I appreciate my small garden space.

Learning how to maximize any small garden space starts with giving thought to balance, ease and beauty, and, as always, right plant, right place. Embracing these general concepts will allow you to fill a small space with all of your ornamental (and edible) favorites!

I had so much fun working with a new client, Toni. She, too, has a small suburban lot but a big appetite for gardening. Toni and I met to discuss design ideas to fill the empty beds she and her husband had created. I always begin with a discussion of four key factors.

▶ **Design Style:** What makes you smile in a garden?

▶ **Favorite Plants:** Are they right for the microclimate of the garden?

▶ **Maintenance Practices:** How do you have minimum maintenance with maximum benefit?

▶ **Ornamentals and Edibles:** How can you have the best of both worlds?

After I sketched a design for Toni, the first words out of her mouth were, "I did not know I could have all these beautiful plants!" To which I replied, "Small does not mean you have to do without."

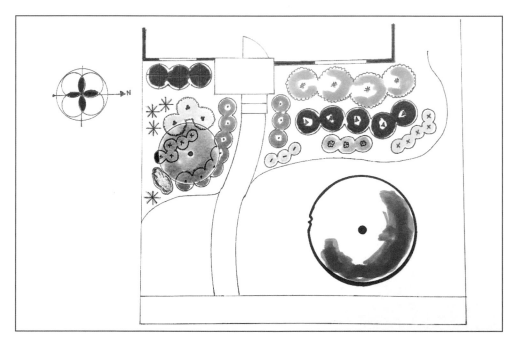

Bring on the Plants, Lose the Weeds!

When we were talking about achieving minimum maintenance, Toni's husband brought up the subject of weed control. I didn't skip a beat, and explained how a densely planted bed can limit or even eliminate the growth of weeds. I illustrated this with a story about another client's terrible weed problem:

During the dog days of a recent summer, my crew and I were tending a large garden that had very little plant material – the beds were nearly empty except for a thin layer of mulch and an unbelievable amount of weeds: every kind you could think of, big and small – a gardener's nightmare. And because the weather was humid and unbearable, it felt like I was yanking weeds from concrete. Needless to say, the work was grueling. All the while, I knew these garden beds screamed for lots of plants – which I soon installed. After all the agony, I was able to give my client a beautiful, essentially weed-free, low-maintenance garden. (See page 102 for some seriously effective tricks for preventing and eradicating these pesky plants.)

If you want to reduce your weeding chores, fill up your garden beds!

Overgrown...or Lush?

As I grow older, I anticipate that my abilities and my stamina to garden may change. A shift in gardening practices and chores is inevitable. Someday in the future, I may not be able to haul barrows of mulch and compost, plant 300-pound trees, or rip out old shrubs to install new ones. I accept these changes but I am unwilling to resign from enjoying my gardens. It is my sincere hope and desire to be in my garden until I am not. Until then, I am excited to share with you helpful ways to minimize chores while maximizing your gardening experiences.

We have explored many ways to design and promote sustainability in the garden. Now, let's look at how to design and promote sustainability on a more personal level: for the gardener.

How can you continue to grow and sustain yourself to ensure many more fruitful and joyful years working in your gardens with comfort and ease? How can your workload lessen without having to compromise experiences and passion?

As I remarked earlier, I have noticed that whatever stage of life my clients are in, young and old alike, none have ever asked for a high maintenance garden – but rather comfort and ease. No matter how much free time and capacity a person has, laborious garden tasks may lead to gardening burnout. As kindred spirits, we want to spend time "putzing" in our gardens, exploring and indulging ourselves in the wonders of nature.

So, how can you embrace comfort and ease in the garden? How can you reduce laborious chores in exchange for lovely, lush gardens you can enjoy without all the work? I'm glad I asked!

Let's start by considering the concept of overgrown versus lush. For some gardeners, red flags shoot up like rockets if they see plants touching one another. Something must be wrong; the gardens are out of sync – or worse, out of control. Panic sets in if plants have taken it upon themselves to co-mingle. I completely understand the feeling of overwhelm and loss of control. Wrong plants in the wrong place can easily become problematic.

All of these shrubs have been planted too close to the house, and to each other

Overgrown gardens differ substantially from lush gardens. When I think of an overgrown garden, I think of plants intruding on one another – impeding one's ability to grow adequately. There is a feeling of confinement and restriction.

Overgrown example #1: Two mature ornamental shrubs have grown into an unintended evergreen hedge because one was planted too close to the other. As a result, the evergreens have "died out" on the impeding side. The plants no longer complement each other; the health and well-being of one or both is compromised.

Overgrown example #2: Many times, trees and shrubs planted too close to a home, garage or shed become overgrown for the space and pose a structural problem. So the plant is pruned or hedged to accommodate the space. Has this happened to you? If so, a reasonable option is to remove the plant or hire a professional to remove it. If you decide to take out the overgrown plant, you will be amazed at, first, the amount of space the plant took up and, second, the possibilities to plant something new and different!

Plants in a lush garden gracefully connect with each other at their mature size. There is no infringement on one or the other, but a sense of connection and continuity. In other words, they play nicely together and choke out weeds because they don't leave open spaces for weeds to thrive in. Lush gardens produce plants that are healthy, not lacking required resources like sun, light, water and air circulation. Lush gardens do not have to be exotic or expensive.

My theory: lush, not overgrown, gardens mean fewer weeds (less work), an elimination of mulch (an added expense), less maintenance (more time to relax), and a calm and inviting feel (for you and your gardens).

Perhaps you will take a moment to assess your gardens. Is there a healthy existence between the plants? Are your gardens lush or overgrown?

A Case Study

One day I received a call from a new client, Pat, who was very concerned about her gardens. She was worried they were overgrown, out-of-control, and she would not be able to maintain them any longer. Upon arrival at her home, I moseyed off to the backyard to steal a quick look. I saw beautiful, lush garden beds – most of them densely planted. I also noticed that other beds had mysterious, large empty spots.

Pat and I began assessing her gardens. She told me that she had recently lost her husband, her garden sidekick, her better half – which had prompted her call to me. It was obvious she and her husband had worked avidly together to create a gorgeous outdoor space. Pat wanted to honor her husband by keeping the gardens up as they always had together.

As we strolled together through her gardens, I asked about those empty spots in some of the beautiful beds, which were sprouting weeds like crazy. Pat explained that many perennials had been dug out, mostly Hosta, in the last few weeks. She felt her gardens were overcrowded and might cause her unnecessary garden maintenance in the future, so she hosted a "digging out" party for family and friends. It was obvious that in just a short time weeds had started to take over where the Hosta had once been.

There's no room for weeds to grow through this cover of various Hostas

I shared my theory about "overgrown versus lush," and how I felt lush was lovely, low maintenance, and an advantage in the garden. Pat welcomed the idea as I pointed out where the weeds were growing and where they were not. She realized her lush garden beds (fully planted, without too much space between) showed no signs of weeds, even though she had not weeded in a few weeks. The only place weeds were growing was in the areas where plants had been dug up.

My solution: If Pat wanted lower maintenance gardens, the solution was simple: divide and transplant the many gorgeous remaining Hosta and fill up the empty spaces in her beds where the weeds were growing.

More about my theory: In the natural ecosystem no one is dividing and thinning plants to remedy or prevent overcrowding. Nature takes care of itself without our intervention and thrives magnificently. I believe plants, like people, are meant to touch. We all know how powerful and impactful the human touch can be; I do not think it is any different for plants. Imagine working hard to grow in life (as we all do) and never touching anyone or anything. Plants co-mingling side by side in the garden create synergy and communion, which is ultimately received by us.

I have not always felt this deep relationship with plants and the relationship they share with each other. Once upon a time I was the exhausted gardener dividing plants for no rhyme or reason. I recklessly planted, dug up, divided and planted again; it was an unrewarding, vicious circle. Today, I have a greater appreciation for letting things be without interruption. As a result, I am happier (and healthier) watching my gardens grow and evolve naturally.

A Shout-Out to Groundcover

I'm such a strong believer in the benefits of heavily planted garden beds. Did you know that groundcovers are a straight ticket to less maintenance? They are meant to cover the ground, so do not be alarmed when they start spreading – that's their job!

Pachysandra is a beautiful groundcover – perfect for low maintenance gardens

The Joy of Container Gardening

Because of the huge variety of containers available today, containers are one of the most useful, effective elements of a small-space garden. They act to provide color, texture, dimension, elevation and even art. They can be arranged within a garden bed, on a patio or deck, at the front entrance – almost anywhere. A few more things I love about container gardening: the ease of moving them around (especially if they have wheels), and the ability to garden without bending or squatting.

Garden Myth: Put small rocks in the bottom of your containers.

Not true! Rocks act as a holding tank for water and will eventually rot the roots of a plant (it smells awful, too) – the complete opposite of the intent to create good drainage. The best and only planting medium you'll need for your containers is organic potting soil.

Container Tips

- Before planting, gently loosen the roots of container plants.
- Line your container with a disposal diaper. It will hold water and steadily release it to your plants.
- Put a coffee filter on the bottom of your container to keep the soil from washing away through the drainage hole.
- You must have good drainage in potting containers or your plants will get root rot.
- Protect porous outdoor containers from heaving and cracking in winter by covering with a plastic bag filled with mulch, straw, or leaves. It is also a good idea to raise them off the ground with bricks or wood.

Combine colorful foliage with flowers in containers

My garden friend Christina Salwitz, author of *Fine Foliage: Elegant Plant Combinations for Garden and Container,* is magnificent at creating breathtaking containers filled with color, texture and interest. Here are a few of her favorite container gardening secrets:

Mix up container plants with different textures and colors

- **Know the expected lifespan for the container planting.** Make sure that you know exactly how long you intend to keep the container planted with the combination you create. Most designs should be planted densely to look rich and abundant. If it is a short-term container design for a season or two, pack it REALLY full. If it is more long term, leave some room for things to fill out.

- **Choose the right shape container to suit the plants you are using.** For a long term planting like a Japanese maple (which will need some soil maintenance and pruning to its lateral roots) never put it in a container with a shoulder or a belly shape, as it will restrict your access.

- **Follow the rule of three: three heights, three textures and three colors.** This is a great all around basic rule for most designs. Unless you are creating a monochromatic design, which is also excellent, the rule of three is an easy way to plan your planting. Also, be sure to think about the way that the container will be viewed. If it sits against a wall or corner, then there is no reason to have one element centered with everything dancing around it. Center right or center left can be just as much if not more effective in designing the layout for a container.

If It Can Hold Soil, It's a Planter!

One of my favorite things to do is to reuse whatever I can, whenever I can. Any day that we reuse something and keep it out of a landfill is a good day. This especially holds true for the garden. In case you haven't noticed, there's a new sensation that's sweeping the garden nation: if it can hold soil, it's a planter! Let's hear it for upcycling.

Gone are the days of using only traditional "plant" containers. Selecting unexpected or found objects as planters adds fun, character and interest to the garden. Not only will your gorgeous plantings stand out, but so will the whimsical container in which they're planted!

The world is your oyster when it comes to unconventional planting vessels, and I encourage you to use as many funky, madcap containers as you can get your hands on – within limits, of course! Once you've trained your eye and mind to think out of the box (literally), your creative juices will start flowing. In my ventures, I've stumbled upon quite a few eccentric receptacles, so I've compiled a list of just some of the things I've seen (or used!) as planters. But let me warn you, the list of quirky planters goes on and on. Suddenly, before you know it, everything becomes a planter, both in- and outdoors.

Shoe	Bathtub	Wheelbarrow
Toy truck	Galvanized tub	Baby carriage
Toilet	Vintage cans	Sink
Mailbox	Tree stump	Vintage kettle
Tackle box	Colander	

Small Space, Big Impact

Ann is a lovely client of mine who resides in a small condominium. Her entrance provides a very small space to garden but she has done a wonderful job creating beautiful, lush shade beds. Not only in-ground plants, but many colorful and creative containers occupy the space. There is an immediate feeling of tranquility. She also incorporated different objects she collected at local art fairs and a soothing water fountain.

A small backyard, such as Ann's above, can feature a variety of lush plants to create a beautiful landscape

The space to the rear of her condo is also very small but that did not stop her desire for more. She wanted to create the same atmosphere in back as she did in her entrance. As the photo shows, the number of plants is limited but the impact is not! She will enjoy lovely four-season interest while snuggled on her couch with her favorite book and a cup of hot tea.

Do You Garden Within a Homeowners Association?

One of my favorite client memories is of Sandra, her gardens and spunky personality. Sandra lived in a condominium with an outdated landscape that looked like all the others. Her space was limited, and also limited by the rules imposed on residents by the Homeowners Association when it came to enhancing their outdoor space. For the record, small space designing is not challenging but sometimes restrictions out of our control can put a damper on the creative design process, unless you're working with someone like Sandra.

Sandra had big dreams and big ideas, despite the written HOA rule not to plant any farther than six feet from the home. Six feet, that's all? In the gardening world, that's nothing – in fact, that's one shrub – hardly a landscape. The six-foot rule (and all the others) did not stop Sandra.

She decided to proceed as if there were no rules. I loved that she did not settle, knew what she wanted, and was ready to go for it.

Her new landscape design included big curvy bedlines, gorgeous ornamental trees, flowering shrubs and evergreens – all intended to fill her small garden space like no other. Honestly, that was the easy part. Now Sandra had to present the design to the board of directors for their approval; we all had our fingers (and toes) crossed and were ready for any rebuttals, if necessary.

Sandra's front yard features curved beds filled with trees, colorful shrubs and flowers

A few days later I received a call from Sandra that I will never forget: "Jan, the board of directors have a request…" Right away, I assumed they said no way, doesn't look like the others, blah, blah, blah. Sandra continued, "just one request: I have to invite them to my first garden party!" We were both overjoyed with the outcome. Sandra was getting her new (bigger) beautiful gardens. And the best part was what I learned from Sandra: no doesn't always mean no – at least when it comes to making an outdoor space more attractive. It's okay to push the envelope, because sometimes people don't know what's available until someone else shows them differently. Today, Sandra's gardens are more gorgeous than ever and remind me of her big, beautiful personality!

This is the other side of Sandra's front yard, featuring more beautiful beds of trees, shrubs and flowers

SIX

ORDERLY CHAOS

a perennial garden makeover and tips for plant selection

*We learn from our gardens to deal with the most urgent question
of the time: how much is enough?*

~WENDELL BERRY

Have you ever visited a garden that felt chaotic, thrown together or unkempt? This can happen in gardens that don't give you the sense of balance, ease and beauty. Maybe your eye doesn't know where it should look because of all the different colors, textures and heights. In fact, when there is a lot of color happening in a space, it can seem overwhelming and over stimulating. Like many gardeners, I love variety in the garden, but I also want that variety – that chaos – to be *orderly*.

A Chaotic Shade Garden Gets a Simple Makeover

I received a call from a client who was concerned about her very large shade garden. Gail told me that despite her many design attempts with beautiful shade loving perennials, the garden was unfulfilling, lacked appeal and looked too busy. What could she do?

When I arrived at Gail's house, the garden bed was indeed quite large and housed a large number and variety of plants. To be sure, the garden felt and appeared chaotic and unbalanced. Perennials were planted here, there and everywhere – without apparent rhyme or reason. Petite plants were obscured behind more substantial plants and vice-versa. Though you may be asking, "What's wrong with that? I like the wild effect," Well, there is nothing truly *wrong* at all, but a little tweaking in the garden can go a long long way.

A few of the perennials that were dug up and rearranged in the shade garden

A simple solution. The solution was instantly clear to me and the approach simple. All I had to do was tweak some things. Gail did not have to buy any more plants; she had plenty to work with already.

To start, I laid out a tarp, dug up all the perennials and grouped like plants together on the tarp. My next step was to replant everything, but tweak their arrangement. I started planting the tallest perennials in the back of the garden bed. Once in the ground again, they spread beautifully across the back of her garden, creating a pleasing height and flow.

Next, the medium-size plants claimed the middle row. Again, I grouped like plants together. Finally, I bordered the shade garden bed with shorter shade perennials.

Shade-Loving Perennials in Gail's Garden

(Zone 5b, hardy down to -15 to -10 F)

Tall

- *Matteuccia struthiopteris* Ostrich Fern (Zones 3-7S/9W)
- *Hosta fortunei* Plantain Lily (Zones 3-9)
- *Ligularia dentate* 'Britt-Marie Crawford' (Zones 4-9)
- *Hosta* 'Sum and Substance' (Zones 4-9)
- *Astilbe* 'Straussenfeder' Ostrich Plume (Zones 3-8)
- *Cimiciuga ramose* 'Hillside Black Beauty' (Zones 4-8)

Hosta 'Sum and Substance'

Medium

- *Hakonechloa macra* 'All Gold' (Zones 4-9)
- *Hosta* 'Patriot' (Zones 4-8)
- *Helleborus* 'Walhelivor' Ivory Prince (Zones 6-8S/9W)
- *Dicentra spectabilis* Pink Bleeding Heart (Zones 3-9)
- *Polystichum acrostichoides* Christmas Fern (Zones 4-8)

Hakonechloa macra

Shorter

- *Athyrium niponicum* 'Pictum' Japanese Painted Fern (Zones 5-8)
- *Astilbe chinensis* 'Visions' (Zones 4-8)
- *Brunnera macrophylla* 'Jack Frost' (Zones 3-8)
- *Heuchera* 'Georgia Peach' (Zones 4-9)
- *Heuchera* 'Palace Purple' (Zones 4-9)
- *Hosta* 'Fire and Ice' (Zones 4-8)
- *Asarum europaeum* European Wild Ginger (Zones 5-8S/9W)

Brunnera macrophylla

In Gail's redesign, I intentionally placed a very dark foliage plant like 'Britt-Marie Crawford' Ligularia next to the very bright and brilliant-colored leaf of 'Sum and Substance' Hosta. Creating this type of color contrast in the garden is aesthetically pleasing and captivating.

Once everything was planted and mulched, we stepped back and admired the vast difference in the "new" shade garden. There was a beautiful flow and a new feeling of balance and comfort in its complexity. We had attained an essential simplicity. The different textures and colors complemented each plant with intention. Gail immediately saw (and felt) the difference and fell in love with her newly reorganized shade garden. Redesigning before buying allowed Gail to purchase more plants for another garden bed. Our work is never done, is it?

To go from chaotic to orderly, it takes a little planning. If you are considering a new garden or renovating an existing one, I recommend creating an inventory list of existing plants and categorizing them by color and size. Plot on paper how you might lay the plants out differently to create a fresh and unexpected feel in the garden; this process can get you to another level of enjoyment with your garden. Do not forget spacing to avoid overcrowding and future challenges in the garden. Always check plant tags for spacing guides or do an online search. Though I like to have plants growing close to one another for effect and to keep weeds at bay, you must remember that it is of vital importance to give each plant enough space to grow and mature properly.

Many perennials can be easily divided and transplanted in the garden. Spring and autumn are ideal times to divide and plant. I encourage you to rethink before buying. Recycling (and saving money) is a good garden habit to have!

A Little Help from My Friends

As you know, I garden in the Detroit area, Zone 5b. Let me introduce you to two of my garden expert friends who garden in different parts of the U.S., where winters are warmer. You have already met Christina Salwitz, who gave us her design tips for containers in Chapter 5. She is The Personal Garden Coach in the Seattle area and is co-author of *Fine Foliage*. Jenny Nybro Peterson, lives in Austin, Texas, and is the author of *The Cancer Survivor's Garden Companion* and co-author of *Indoor Plant Décor*. Christina and Jenny, along with other expert gardening friends, will be contributing gardening tips and lists of their favorite, easy-to-grow plants as we go along.

Christina Salwitz's top five low maintenance perennials
(Seattle area)

Sedum

- *Hypericum* 'Ignite Scarlet' (Zones 5-9)
- *Epimedium* Barrenwort (Zones 4-9)
- *Hardy Geranium* 'Rozanne' or 'Johnson's Blue' (Zones 4-9)
- *Lavender* 'Phenomenal' (Zones 4-8)
- *Sedum* 'Angelina' (Zones 3-11)

Jenny Nybro Peterson's top five low maintenance perennials
(Austin area)

Lantana

- *Lantana* spp. (Zones 9-11)
- *Salvia leucantha* Mexican Bush Sage (Zones 8-10)
- *Tagetes lucida* Mexican Mint Marigold (Zones 8-11)
- *Muhlenbergia dumosa* 'Bamboo Muhly' (Zones 7-10)
- *Verbena Canadensis* 'Homestead Purple' (Zones 7-11)

Five more low maintenance perennials in varying hardiness zones:

Coral Bell

- *Heuchera micrantha* Coral Bell 'Palace Purple' (Zones 4-8)
- *Melampodium leucanthum* Black Foot Daisy (Zones 5-10)
- *Salvia* 'Pozo Blue' Hybrid Musk Sage (Zones 7-10)
- *Vernonia lindheimeri* var. *leucophylla* Silver Ironweed (Zones 6-10)
- *Phlomis russeliana* Hardy Jerusalem Sage (Zones 4-10)

When a Bargain Plant is Not a Bargain...and why I don't "settle"

While we are on the topic of plant inventory: who doesn't like a great sale, right? The end of the growing season inevitably offers alluring plant deals like buy one get one free, 50% off, or three for the price of one. It's awfully tempting to stock up and figure out later where to plant these "deals of the day"! Sadly, I always find the remains of dried-up potted sale plants tucked away in clients' yards because someone did not know what to do with these little gems once they got them home. Many times we can get a great deal, but even this cheap gardener is going to caution you to think before you buy because I'm guilty as charged. Here's my story:

A trip to Paris with friends touring many lovely gardens left me incredibly intrigued and inspired. I especially love how Europeans use evergreens in the landscape and to dress up window boxes and containers. When I returned home, I was on a mission to recreate the look and the joie de vivre – joy of life – feeling I had in Paris. My goal was to create a formal look in my window boxes using evergreens, so I was in the market to purchase twelve small boxwoods.

And then it was my lucky day. A local nursery was advertising a sale on the radio: four boxwoods for $12.00. Excited about this nearly too-good-to-be-true deal for my Paris-inspired window boxes, I raced to the garden center, adrenaline flowing.

I sprinted through the doors of the nursery as soon as I arrived, my eyes darting across the store in pursuit of the – no, *my* – boxwoods. As I hunted, my head was swimming with sensational thoughts and ideas of an entire Parisian

Lovely boxwood plants in Paris

garden; the boxwoods would just be the beginning. And then I saw them. The shimmering aura I'd put around the fabulous evergreens in my head vanished. My heart sank as I gazed upon the smallest, most itsy bitsy, irregular-shaped boxwoods I had ever seen. Pallets next to the display proudly propped up a handwritten sign: *Sale of the Century: 4 for $12.* I mumbled to myself, *You're kidding me.* It would take no less than five years before I could actually enjoy them in my window boxes, if they even made it that long. I left the nursery, boxwood-less and defeated.

> **LESSON LEARNED:** Purchasing plants only because they are a good deal leads to low value gardening – to "settling." I have learned in my second half of life that settling in the garden leaves me feeling disappointed and frustrated.
>
> **BIG QUESTION:** How do you know if you are getting a healthy plant and your money's worth? You inspect, then select.

Inspecting Before Selecting

Tips for finding a healthy plant:

- **Examine plant leaves.** Do the leaves look healthy? Are there spots, dark areas, holes from insects? Caution: if you pick up a plant and a Japanese beetle or whitefly bolts out of it, put it down.

- **Don't buy the tallest plant on the shelf;** buy the fullest, even if it is shorter. Bigger is not always better.

- **Beware of roots growing out of the bottom of the container** – that is a good indication the plant has been in the pot for quite some time and is probably root-bound.

Inspect plants before you buy them

- **Be wary of small plants in large containers.** They may not have established healthy root systems yet. In fact, sometimes with a larger container all you're getting – and paying for – is more soil and not more plant. Inspect.

▶ **Perform the healthy plant test.** Here's how: First, do not be shy about removing the plant from the container. I do it all the time. In fact, I inspect every plant I purchase for clients; it's the only way to ensure the roots are healthy and ready for transplant. Begin by laying the container on its side and gently tapping it to allow airflow; this will make it easy to remove the plant from the container. When actually removing the plant, pay attention to two things: how difficult it is to get the plant out of the container and if the plant has a root ball or not. If it does not come out of the con-

Healthy rootball

tainer and/or you struggle to remove it, it is probably root-bound – put it back. Conversely, if the plant comes out easily but without a root ball, it has not established healthy roots – put it back. If it glides out easily and the roots are wrapped around, holding in soil, that is a healthy plant. Again, do not be shy. It's your money and you should get the best value when purchasing plants. If a sales associate asks what you are doing, simply say you are inspecting before selecting!

*

We can't always avoid a little chaos in our garden (that's life), but we can go a long way toward orderly chaos by doing thoughtful planning, taking advantage of lessons learned – by others or ourselves – and not letting our emotions lead us too far astray.

We have it in our power to create serenity and simplicity, and in doing so we give ourselves a respite from the often-chaotic world beyond the garden gate. It's a skill and a blessing.

SEVEN

ORNAMENTAL TREES AND SHRUBS
focal point of a harmonious garden

I never saw a discontented tree.

~ JOHN MUIR

In the design of a garden, even a very small garden, I like to include at least one ornamental tree. It adds dimension, shade possibilities, color, texture – and a home for birds, squirrels and a myriad little creatures that give a garden life. For me, a tree has a calming influence. It conveys a sense of quiet, peace and permanence. Did I mention beauty? And then there's a tree's connection with memory: the old swing from our childhood, the sweet cherries we remember picking in the heat of a long-ago summer…

We plant trees for many reasons. When my mother passed away many years ago, I had a strong desire to plant a 'Miss Kim' lilac tree in her memory and honor – and so I did. Years later, I still love the fragrant, dainty tree planted near my front entrance. Each spring, I marvel at the unforgettable perfume and beautiful blossoms that so lovingly remind me of my mother. There is something very special about a small specimen tree in a landscape that becomes personal and treasured for many years.

Ornamental trees are a focal point in a garden, no matter the season

Whether you are selecting a tree to commemorate a special event, to honor a loved one, or for purely aesthetic or practical reasons (tall trees with large canopies to offer shade, dense trees to serve as windbreaks, fruit and nut trees for their yumminess) there is a wide selection of fabulous small ornamental trees to choose from. There's sure to be one to fit your garden and your needs.

Before You Select Your Tree...

Your tree's survival, longevity and landscape value will be enhanced if you first consider site conditions along with the tree's physical and ornamental traits. Below are a few helpful tips to consider the next time you make a small tree purchase!

▸ **Know your zone** and know your tree's zone-hardiness. The U.S. Department of Agriculture's (USDA) hardiness zone map (see page 31) is a great resource and guide to knowing if a plant is well-suited for your area, based on the plant's characteristics on the label.

▶ **Don't forget soil conditions.** Some ornamental trees require specific soil conditions to maintain healthy growth. When in doubt, get a soil test to determine the texture, pH, and nutrient levels of your soil. You can buy an inexpensive soil test kit at your garden center, local County Extension office or Cooperative Extension office.

▶ **Pay attention to drainage.**
Drainage is very important for plant health. Most trees grow best in well-drained, moist (not saturated) soils. Poor drainage will eventually cause trees to die because of insufficient oxygen levels in the soil.

▶ **Take light requirements seriously.**
When I first started gardening, I was certain that plants intended for full sun would likely survive in part shade. *Wrong!* Trees need light to grow…some more than others. Remember that light affects the amount of flowering, fruiting and fall leaf coloration – all significant attributes.

This is a good example of how to plant: the berm is flat on the top, not sloped.

▶ **Be aware of wind and air circulation.** They play key roles in plant survival. Try to evaluate the amount of wind a small tree will be exposed to. Another one of my gardening blunders was planting a small Japanese maple on a northern exposure. After four years, the small tree could not survive the forceful northern cold winds and it eventually died. Another lesson learned.

Favorite Ornamental Trees

Three of My Favorites:
(Detroit area)

- *Amelanchier* × *grandiflora* 'Autumn Brilliance' (Zones 4-9)
- *Cercis canadensis* 'Forest Pansy' (Zones 5-9)
- *Cornus alternifolia* Pagoda Dogwood (Zones 4-8)

From Garden Expert Christina Salwitz:
(Seattle area)

- *Acer palmatum* Japanese Maple (Zones 5-8)
- *Stewartia pseudocamellia* Japanese Stewartia (Zones 5-8)
- *Styrax japonicus* Japanese Snowbell (Zones 5-8)

Serviceberry 'Autumn Brilliance'

From Garden Expert Jenny Nybro Peterson:
(Austin area)

- *Bauhinia lunarioides* 'Anacacho' Orchid (Zone 8)
- *Prunus Mexicana* Mexican Plum (Zones 6-8)
- *Carcis Canadensis* var. *texensis* 'Oklahoma' Redbud (Zones 6-9)

Some beauties for warmer winter zones:

- *Morella cerifera* Wax Myrtle (Zone s7-11)
- *Chamaerops humilis* 'European Fan Palm' (Zones 8-11)
- *Punica granatum* 'Smith' Angel Red® Pomegranate (Zones 7-11)

Japanese Maple

Selecting an appropriate small ornamental tree is as much fun as shopping for new garden implements. Just remember to do your homework!

Some tree planting tips

Ball and burlap trees can be very heavy. Using a tree "ball cart" makes planting much easier.

- When removing a tree from the grow container, never grab and pull at the trunk. Instead, lay the tree on its side and gently press down with your knee to loosen the soil. Roll it around and do this a few time, it will be easier to remove. If the tree or container is too big, cut the container off before planting.

- After you have planted a tree, do not step on the soil around it; by pressing down on the soil around the tree you are compacting it and the air in it is lost.

- An old gardening trick: Before planting your tree, add 10 packages of paper matches and 2 cups of Epsom salt to the soil that will go into the soil around the tree. The matches provide a slow release of sulfur and the Epsom salt provides magnesium: both important for root growth and health.

- Never use paint (or any synthetic material) on torn or peeled bark. Your tree knows how to heal itself.

Why You Shouldn't Stake a Newly Planted Tree

Trees like to shake it to left and shake it to the right, like some of us. They need to be able to swing and sway to develop strong roots. Exception: only stake a tree if it has fallen and needs support or it is very top heavy at the time of planting. Example: a newly planted Hydrangea tree has big blooms and can be top-heavy, so staking is necessary until a strong root system is established and it can hold its own. If you do stake a tree, use a piece of rubber from an old garden hose, to protect the bark.

Snip and Prune

Proper pruning is beneficial to the health and well-being of a tree. So if you or someone else is going to do any pruning, do it this way:

A clean cut. When pruning the branch of a tree, big or small, always cut at the branch collar (where a *branch* joins the trunk). I call this a clean cut. A clean cut on an angle promotes the growth of a callus that seals and protects the wound *naturally*. There is no need to apply a synthetic store-bought dressing to the wound, Mother Nature has this one!

Water shoots and tree suckers. Shoots are vertical growth from the branches of a tree trunk. Suckers grow from the root system of a tree; both zap nutrients from a tree and should be removed. They add no value to the health of a tree and are aesthetically unattractive. Over-pruning, overwatering, diseases, or drought conditions contribute to the growth of shoots and suckers. Some trees are more susceptible than others, so don't fret over shoots and suckers; just keep pruning them. For tips on general garden pruning, see page 99.

Tree suckers grow from the tree's root system

Spring is an ideal time to prune shoots and suckers; I don't wait, I cut them sooner rather than later. Here's how to snip and prune:

▶ **Prune water shoots** as close to the tree trunk as possible, next to the branch collar.

▶ **Prune tree suckers** as close to the base (root) of the tree as possible.

I consider pruning shoots and suckers regular garden maintenance; it is a good practice to get into. You can use a bypass pruner for most shoots and suckers. For large thicker ones, use a lopper; it's easier, so why struggle?

3-Cut Method. This is an excellent way to remove a tree branch that is too large or too heavy to support. Here's how it's done:

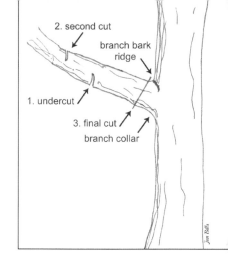

- ▶ **Step 1:** Make a shallow notch on the outside of the branch collar, on the underside of the branch. This first cut will stop the branch from falling and tearing the bark (branches get heavy) as it pulls away from the tree.

- ▶ **Step 2:** The next cut is on the outside of the first cut. Cut through the branch, leaving a small stub.

- ▶ **Step 3:** Make the final cut. Be sure to cut the branch on an angle at the collar so it heals correctly, as shown in the drawing.

Regular shoot and sucker pruning will keep your trees healthy and attractive. Plus, it allows you to get up close and personal, maybe that's how the term "tree huggers" got started!

Ornamental Shrubs

We all have our favorite ornamental shrubs in the garden – think Hydrangeas, Dogwood, Azaleas and Roses. They bring reliable color year after year and help us to create a pleasing, harmonious palette. The choices are endless. Based on right plant, right place, here are a few of my "tried and true" plants I use in my own and my clients' gardens. As you can see by the range of zones for each of the plants below, some of them are hardy down to zone 2 and others up to zone 9. So there should be something for most garden environments. If in doubt, check the zone map for your specific area.

- ▶ **Pruning:** Ornamental shrubs require little to no pruning. For easy pruning tips, see page 99.

> **Shrub:** a woody plant, smaller than a tree, with several stems or branches arising near the base or at ground level.
>
> *(Garden-pedia)*

Favorite Ornamental Shrubs

Small garden shrubs:

- *Fothergilla gardenii* Dwarf Fothergilla (Zones 5-9)
- *Weigela florida* 'Spilled Wine®' (Zones 4-8)
- *Ninebark Physocarpus opulifolious* 'Tiny Wine®' (Zones 3-8)
- *Rosa Meiswetdom* 'Sweet Drift®' Groundcover Rose (Zones 4-10)
- *Hydrangea paniculata* Jane 'Little Lime™' Hardy Hydrangea (Zones 3-8)

Ninebark

Large garden shrubs:

- *Hydrangea paniculata* 'Limelight' Hydrangea (Zones 3-8)
- *Physocarpus oulifolius* 'Center Glow' (Zones 2-8)
- *Sambucus nigra* 'Black Lace™' Elderberry (Zones 4-7)
- *Hydrangea arborescens* 'Incrediball®' Smooth Hydrangea (Zones 3-9)
- *Cornus alba* 'Elegantissima' Red Twig Dogwood (Zones 2-8)

Red Twig Dogwood

Evergreens:

- *Thuja occidentalis* 'Little Giant' Dwarf Arborvitae (Zones 3-8)
- *Thuja occidentalis* 'Bobozam' Mr. Bowling Ball™ (Zones 3-8)
- *Rhododendron* 'Pink Ruffle' Azalea (Zones 7b-10)
- *Ilex glabra* 'Shamrock' (Zones 4-9)
- *Picea abies Nidiformis* 'Nest Spruce' (Zones 2-8)

Arborvitae

Ornamental Grasses

While you're making your garden beautiful with ornamental trees and shrubs, don't overlook the drop-dead ethereal beauty of ornamental grasses. Here are a few to tempt you:

- *Calamagrostis acutiflora* 'Karl Foerster' Feather Reed Grass (Zones 4-9)
- *Festuca glauca* 'Elijah' Blue Fescue (Zones 4-11)
- *Hakonechloa macra* 'All Gold' Hakone Grass (Zones 5-9)
- *Pennisetum orientale* 'Karley Rose' Oriental Fountain Grass (Zones 5-10)
- *Pennisetum alopecuroides* 'Hameln' Dwarf Fountain Grass (Zones 4-11)

'Karley Rose' Oriental Fountain Grass

Deciding when to remove a plant. I'm such a huge fan of trees and shrubs and grasses, and all growing things. But (true confession) in the second half of my life, if there is a plant in my garden that I no longer adore, am not drawn to, was put in the "wrong" place and failed to thrive – or that no longer serves wildlife, the environment or myself – I remove it. Gone are the days of tolerance for the sake of tolerance. It's part of my liberating philosophy. If you have a problematic plant, you shouldn't feel like a murderer for removing it from the garden. Give it your blessing and gratitude and send it off to a friend or to become compost for other plants. It's the circle of life.

EIGHT

THE FLOW OF WATER
the essential element in a thriving garden

⁘

If there is magic on the planet, it is contained in the water.
~ LOREN EISELEY

The growing season is a time for fertility. It is a time when everything comes alive, a time for rejuvenation, a time to celebrate. But nothing thrives or stays refreshed, including us, without water.

Of course we like to have a garden that feels lush. We want our plants to be happy. One of my most frequently asked questions is when to water plants and how much – for good reason: effective watering practices are critical to sustain healthy landscapes and gardens. Irrigation is *extremely* important and the key to having healthy plants and trees. So how do you know when your gardens need a little refreshment?

As a landscape professional, it is difficult for me to recommend a single "standard" watering program for new gardens due to variations in soil conditions, natural precipitation, temperature and a plant's own moisture. However, all these factors must be considered before irrigating your new gardens. Oddly enough, *overwatering* is the most common cause of death for newly planted trees and shrubs. Rest assured, by applying the right plant, right place concept and a proper watering schedule, you will enjoy your landscape and gardens for many years to come.

Quick Test to Know When You Need to Water:

Start by carefully digging 6-8 inches near the root zone of a plant and squeeze a handful of soil. If the soil is damp enough to form a ball, no water is necessary. On the other hand, if the soil falls apart easily, it is definitely time to water. Do not worry if the top few inches of soil are dry. If you observe that a plant's foliage looks dry and crispy on the edges, it's likely that it needs a drink.

These leaves indicate that the plant needs watering

But if foliage turns yellow and wilts, it's a sign that it's been overwatered and saturated – even though it appears to be thirsty.

Why you don't want to overwater: A plant's roots need just as much air as they do moisture: overwatering will saturate the soil, drive out the air and suffocate the roots.

This may seem counterintuitive, but trust me: deep, infrequent watering encourages roots to grow and spread into the soil for maximum plant growth and health. Superficial watering (on tops of plants) offers no rewards because the water does not penetrate the root system – and usually water is wasted.

To prevent fungus and disease, always water the soil at the base of the plant, *not the leaves.*

Mulch: My Best Garden Friend

Mulch is a key ingredient in your garden that will ensure healthy, well-established plants and trees. After you've watered (the roots, not the leaves!), it's important to keep the soil moist. To do this, use a top dressing – in other words, mulch. My favorite mulches are shredded hardwood, shredded leaves, wood chips and pine needles. Mulch not only helps retain moisture, it minimizes weeds, adds nutrients to the soil as it decomposes, saves on maintenance and is attractive in the garden. All new plantings should be mulched, not only for moisture retention, but it also protects their young, shallow roots during cold winter months.

To get your new plants off to a healthy start:

▶ **Layer the mulch** at least 3-4 inches thick. Don't be shy – it decomposes over time.

▶ **Never lay mulch against tree trunks** or woody ornamental shrubs (this is called "volcano" mulching). Mulch should be at least two inches away from a tree trunk. It's very helpful to create a "well" around the tree trunk and the base of the shrub to capture and hold in water.

Lay down a layer of cardboard before you mulch to suppress any weeds

- **Lift and spread.** Always lift the branches and foliage as you spread the mulch under it.
- **Do not let mulch lie on top branches or foliage;** it will burn them.

You can protect delicate perennials from damage when dumping mulch in your garden beds by covering the plants with containers or buckets. Simply dump the mulch, spread, and lift up the buckets. Ta-da! This method is one of my favorite dirty little secrets and it works brilliantly!

Mulch Myths:

- **Mulch attracts carpenter ants, termites and other undesirables.** Not true! Pests are not attracted to mulch. Actually, the mulch is an insect repellant. Use mulch, lots of it.

- **Mulch robs soil of nutrients.** Not true! Actually it is quite the opposite. As mulch breaks down, it adds nutrients to the soil. Mulch your garden beds well; you'll be glad you did.

When "Free" Isn't Such a Good Thing

I would caution you about mulching your garden beds with free wood chips from tree companies or city municipal services. Trees are often removed due to disease. Adding this type of mulch to your garden beds may invite unwanted pests and diseases. I do, however, think it is beneficial and economical to use free wood chips in areas where there are no plantings – like a pathway or driveway.

Compost: My Other Best Garden Friend

I always use organic compost to enrich soil and feed plants, instead of synthetic soil amendments and fertilizers. Composting is an ideal way to recycle waste. It can be as simple as making a pile of leaves and letting them sit there to decompose. Plus, composting at home is free! Following are unusual items to add to your compost bin:

Fireplace ashes	Dryer lint
Clean cloth rags	Vacuum cleaner debris
Used paper towels	Cotton swabs – without chemicals
Human and animal hair	Corks
Cardboard egg cartons	Nail clippings (toes, too)
Paper rolls	

The only thing I use to fertilize my gardens is organic compost. If a plant needs anything unusual to grow and thrive, I won't buy it.

Irrigation Systems

Permanent Irrigation Systems

Permanent irrigation for garden beds can be costly and wasteful. Time and time again I witness water being wasted and misused. Irrigation systems are dispersing water in all the wrong places.

Before the water has a chance to penetrate the soil, it typically evaporates in the air (especially on very hot days) or ends up on the leaves of plants, not the root systems, or down a city storm drain.

If you have an existing overhead watering system, you may want to consider converting it to a mister for better efficiency. Also, changing your watering schedule can reduce your water bill considerably. Established gardens that are well mulched require little watering.

Watering Tip

Newly planted gardens in many regions need an effective watering schedule the first growing season to ensure healthy root systems. Mature, established landscapes and gardens do not need constant watering unless there is a severe drought situation.

Drip Irrigation

For anyone considering an irrigation system, I recommend the drip method. Water flows directly into the soil, dispersing and hydrating the roots where needed. There is virtually no waste. The water lines are wrapped around the base of the plants and covered with a layer of mulch such as shredded hardwood, pine bark, shredded leaves or pine straw. A drip irrigation system is a simple and effective watering method that can be successfully installed in your gardens.

Water Harvesting

As a gardener, I am intrigued with the flow of water (or lack of) on clients' properties – and how that water can be harvested and kept from being lost. Many downspouts empty down the driveway into city storm drains instead of back into the gardens.

Ideally, a drainage pipe from the downspout redirects the water to another area where a "pop-up" releases the water. An inexpensive way to redirect water away from your home and into your gardens is with vinyl accordion-type downspout extensions. I like these because they bend easily, can be buried if desired – and are cheap! One objective to water harvesting is to keep water out of storm drains, allowing it to permeate back into the earth where it belongs. Consider walking your property to observe where water is flowing from downspouts. Are there ways you can redirect water back into your gardens and out of city storm drains?

Catch Basins for Downspouts

Proper drainage is critical. Over time, drainage pipes clog from years of gutter debris accumulation leading to reduced drainage efficiency. A catch basin filters drainage pipes and reduces clogged downspouts – eliminating drainage problems and allowing proper entry to clean out accumulated debris. I highly recommend installing catch basins on downspouts, whenever possible.

Water harvesting is an excellent way to reduce water usage and costly water bills during the growing season. Not only that, it can have a major impact on the environment and is extremely beneficial to our natural waterways. And it helps keep thirsty plants healthy, too!

A Few Popular Water Harvesting Methods

▷ **Rain gardens** are very useful for the home gardener, especially if you have a shallow area that collects problematic water accumulation. Desirable plantings for rain gardens include deep-rooted native plants and ornamental grasses. Runoff sources like downspouts and driveways can be ideal locations for rain gardens.

▷ **Rain chains** divert water the same way traditional boring ho-hum downspouts do. They are easy to attach to a gutter or eaves. And not only is a rain chain functional, it looks and sounds lovely as the water cascades down it.

▷ **Rain barrels** are a great way to harvest water for free, aside from the cost of the barrel. The barrel options are many, from very basic and simple to the elaborate and attractive rain barrels available at local hardware stores and garden centers. But you can surf the internet to find sources and DIY sites on how to assemble your own. However, in some states, it is unlawful to capture rainwater. Crazy, I know! You can read more about State Rainwater Harvesting Laws and Legislation at http://www.ncsl.org.

▷ **Capturing water runoff and redirecting it** is a big one, as mentioned above. Redirecting water to your plants creates a win-win; you don't have to turn on your hose.

▷ **Permeable surfaces** (as shown in the photo, left) for parking lots, driveways, patios, and sidewalks are gaining momentum with homeowners and businesses. Traditional concrete or asphalt surfaces do not allow rainwater to seep into the earth, where it should go. Permeable surfaces can be made of stone or concrete pavers, gravel, cut stone (to look like cobblestone) and a number of new, aesthetically interesting interlocking stone and concrete systems that let water seep into the cracks and not run away from your property. Permeable surfaces are near and dear to my heart. I have replaced most of my concrete surfaces with permeable alternatives. I have one more surface to tackle, my driveway. My plan is to remove the poured concrete and lay crushed fieldstone, which is a fraction of the cost and much more beneficial to the environment.

Gardening Where Water is Scarce:
Xeriscaping

If you live in a region that is impacted by recurring or constant drought conditions, native and drought tolerant plants to the rescue! Your local County Extension Office or Cooperative Extension Office is a wealth of knowledge and an excellent resource for native plants in your region. For so many reasons (not always about water scarcity), people are discovering the benefits and beauty of native plants. They are the favorites of pollinators, and heaven knows, we want to help those important little guys.

> **Xeriscaping:** Designing a landscape and/or garden with the purpose of reducing or eliminating the need for irrigation or additional water to keep plants alive. *(Garden-pedia)*

If you have a limited water supply, water harvesting is an almost essential practice. A companion practice – and one that is very popular lately – is xeriscaping. Here, the emphasis is on designing for water conservation, not specifically on using native plants, though they are usually part of the picture. There are many areas of North America where water availability is restricted or limited. Fortunately, Mother Nature has provided us with a cornucopia of plants that thrive in drier climates. If xeriscaping isn't a familiar term, you might have heard it called smart gardening, water-wise gardening, water-conserving landscaping or drought-tolerant gardening.

Garden Myth: Drought tolerant plants are great because you don't have to water them. Not true! All plants need water, especially the first year they are planted. Water helps plants develop healthy root systems. Drought tolerant plants don't need as much water as the others, but they still need a drink when they are dry.

This landscape features drought-resistant plants

My friend Jenny Peterson is a xeriscape landscape design expert from Austin, Texas. Nearly all of her clients have asked about or installed xeriscape gardens in the past few years.

Here's to more and better ways to keep our water flowing where it can do the most good – for our plants, ourselves and our beautiful planet.

NINE

TEND, DON'T TOIL

more tips on perennials, ornamental shrubs and pruning

❦

Every garden is a chore sometimes,
but no real garden is nothing but a chore.

~ NANCY GRASBY

One of my biggest goals in writing this book is to share ways to reduce repetitive garden chores and increase your level of relaxation. Let's start with perennials. I believe that there can be such a thing as too many perennials in a garden.

My Beef with Perennials

I love perennials, really. They are like the pillows on a sofa that add texture, pops of color and elements of surprise. So why would I be here recommending that you reduce the amount of perennials in your garden bed? Simple…it's because many perennials require cutting, trimming, pruning

and deadheading (continuous care and upkeep) to maintain their beauty and size. It has been my experience through the years that garden beds full of perennials are high maintenance. I use them sparingly in garden plans I design for clients; they are incorporated into the plan as accent plants, not focal points or foundation plantings.

A Cautionary Tale of a High Maintenance Perennial Garden

One of my clients had major surgery in autumn and needed a helping hand in the garden during her recovery period. Sally has big, lovely perennial gardens that fill an entire suburban yard, front and back. They are gorgeous to look at but not classified as low maintenance. As my team of gardeners and I began cutting back Sally's large perennial beds filled with Japanese Anemone, Baptisia, and Bee Balm, to name a few, it was obvious why she needed backup. Who wouldn't? Four gardeners worked five hours for a total of 20 man-hours cutting back her perennials. Twenty hours may not seem like a lot, until it's time to do the work. Whether perennials are cut back in autumn or in spring, this necessary garden chore has to be done.

Low Maintenance Perennials to Ease the Chores

I'm happy to say that there are many low maintenance perennials to choose from. Here is a list of my top ten perennials that are hardy in a wide range of zones. I especially love these perennials because they are attractive and low maintenance:

- *Rudbeckia hirta* Black-eyed Susan (Zones 3-9)
- *Echinacea* Coneflower (Zones 3-9)
- *Salvia* 'May Night' (Zones 4-9)
- *Heuchera* 'Purple Palace' (Zones 4-8)
- *Sedum spectabile* 'Neon' (Zones 3a-9b)
- *Lavandula angustifolia* 'Big Time Blue' (Zones 5-10)
- *Festuca glauca* 'Beyond Blue' (Zones 4-10)
- *Agastache Kudos* 'Kudos Mountain' (Zones 5-10)
- *Helleborus* x *hybridus* 'Winter Jewels Onyx Odyssey' (Zones 5-10)
- *Gaillardia* x *grandiflora* 'Mesa Peach' (Zones 5-10)

Purple Coneflowers

Pruning and Hedging (if you must)

Tending, not toiling applies to pruning, too. I love pruning for all the right reasons and detest this garden chore for all the right reasons. Pruning to control the size and shape of a plant is something I gave up years ago. It is simply too much work, counterproductive, and not a sustainable practice. When we apply the "right plant, right place" concept, the requirement to prune and hedge is reduced significantly.

My Privet Hedge Story

For years, I maintained a privet hedge in my backyard that required constant care in order to keep it somewhat manageable and aesthetically appealing. Twice each season, my husband would break out the electric hedger and we would go to work (usually in the dog days of summer when temperatures were sweltering.) I dreaded this laborious task like the plague. The amount of waste and effort the hedges created was unconscionable. Back then, I did not fully recognize the impact the labor-intensive hedges had on me; I only knew it was not a sustainable practice and it definitely did not fall under the pleasant garden chore category. I think having a tooth pulled would have been more pleasing!

My solution: Finally one day we decided the hedges had to go and hired someone to tear them out. The once thorn-in-my-side hedges were replaced with a new garden consisting of three *Hydrangea arborescens* 'Incrediball', one *Malus* 'Royal Raindrop' Crabapple tree, one

Replacing labor-intensive hedges with hydrangeas gives low-maintenance color

Hydrangea paniculata 'Vanilla Strawberry', one *Physocarpus oplifolius* 'Coppertina' Ninebark, and three *Hydrangea paniculata* 'Limelight' Hydrangea – a few off my garden favorites. Collectively, they create wonderful four-season color, texture and interest.

Bonus: ornamental shrubs require little to no pruning or hedging other than a bit of the expected (and enjoyable) tender loving care.

When I visit clients who have a similar high maintenance hedge (healthy or otherwise) like mine, they admit it is simply too much work to maintain. There are many sustainable replacement shrubs, like Hydrangea, Viburnum, Ninebark, Dogwood, and Weigela that are low maintenance and stunning in the garden as a single specimen or hedge. Sometimes letting go, without guilt, of plants that no longer serve you well in the garden can be very liberating and rewarding.

When Pruning is Necessary

I am not a big fan of pruning; it is probably my least favorite garden chore. In fact, I believe many shrubs and trees are over-pruned. In most cases, dead, diseased, weak or broken branches can be pruned any time of year. If additional pruning is needed on an ornamental shrub, I encourage you to thin out at the base rather than hedge off the top. It is not only healthier for the plant but more aesthetically pleasing.

Pruning is often necessary to maintain a plant's health and natural beauty. Following are my cutting-edge practices on pruning:

  ▶ **The best time to prune** most plants and trees is when they are dormant; winter or early spring is ideal. This is my favorite time because there are no leaves and it is easy to see the plant's branch structure.

- **Early spring flowering shrubs** should be pruned after they have bloomed, preferably before July 4th. If you prune flowering shrubs or trees, like Lilac and Forsythia, before they have produced blooms, you will forfeit blooms for that season only.

- **Early and late summer flowering shrubs** like Hydrangea and Hibiscus should be pruned in late winter or early spring.

- **Avoid major pruning in late summer and early fall.** Pruning stimulates new growth, which may become damaged by freezing temperature.

- **Consider the natural shape and design** of the plant, unless you are creating an animal topiary for Disneyland!

- **Remove branches** that grow inward, cross over other branches or alter the beauty, shape and appearance.

- **Always prune suckers and water shoots** from the base of a tree and along branches. See page 78 for a diagram and tips.

- **Clean your pruners with bleach** regularly to avoid spreading diseases to the rest of your plants.

TEN

WEED OUT THE WEEDS

3 ways to do it and not lose your cool

*A weed is a plant that has mastered every survival skill
except learning how to grow in rows.*

~ DOUG LARSON

I love the acronym O.W.D. In the garden world, it stands for Obsessive Weeding Disorder. Weeding can be very calming, therapeutic, even spiritual experience. It can stimulate instant gratification – and for many, a profound sense of accomplishment. It can be one of the most rewarding garden chores or one of the most dreaded. Either way, it is a necessary and repetitive garden chore that keeps all gardeners on their toes and knees! Unruly, weed-infested gardens can be extremely challenging even for the most experienced gardener.

If you want to minimize the weeds and maximize your gardening pleasures, this chapter is for you. I will share some of my favorite, proven ways to reduce the constant need to weed.

Tip: always wet your gardens before weeding, or weed after a good rain, as weeds are much easier to pluck out when the soil is wet.

Weed Control #1: Solarization

The first process to battle relentless noxious weeds without breaking your back or your bank is called solarization. This organic and eco-friendly method eliminates the use of harmful herbicides and pesticides. Here's how it works:

Solarization uses a plastic sheet or tarp to capture the heat and energy from the sun, which in turn effects a physical change in the soil without the use of harmful chemicals. With

solarization, soil temperatures are raised to lethal levels for many soil-borne plant pathogens such as fungi, bacteria, and pests as well as weed seeds and seedlings. Soil solarization smothers problem weeds at the surface and wipes out the roots as it produces nitrogen in the soil. How cool is that?

Solarization isn't a "quick fix" but it is non-toxic and environmentally friendly. The best time to solarize soil is during the months when the sun's rays are strongest. Solarization requires a little time and effort on your part but the payoff is well worth it.

You'll need:

- Weed trimmer or mower
- Hose and water source
- Plastic sheet or tarp, which is available in the paint department at hardware stores. I have used old plastic tarps, too.
- Rocks, flagstones, concrete blocks – anything heavy enough to secure the plastic in place

Getting started:

- Clear the area you want to solarize by removing all debris such as twigs and branches.
- Mow down or trim extra tall weeds and grass, then rake the area so the ground is as level as possible.
- Wet the area thoroughly with water and immediately lay the plastic, placing it as close to the soil's surface as possible. Note: seal well, because air pockets will prevent the soil from heating to the necessary maximum temperature.
- Secure the plastic around the entire perimeter with rocks, concrete or blocks.
- Keep the plastic in place for at least eight to twelve weeks, the longer the better.

Voila! Remove the plastic and plant your new weed-free garden bed. After planting, add a thick layer of mulch to the area to suppress new weeds.

Solarization helps to stimulate the release of nutrients from organic matter already present in the soil, a valuable and natural bonus for treating garden soil where trees, shrubs, perennials, herbs and vegetables will be planted.

I have used the solarizing method many times and can attest to its success. Eliminating harmful chemicals from seeping into our watershed, storm drains and the environment is a viable and credible solution worth its weight in gold! I take every opportunity to minimize negative impacts and promote positive ones for the environment and wildlife.

Weed Control #2: Bring Out the Cardboard!

My next recommendation to create comfort and ease in the garden includes cardboard. Hands-down, it is a gardener's best friend. Here's a cardboard story to share:

Reclaiming Roxanne's Gardens

A visit to Roxanne's gardens on a beautiful warm Sunday morning clearly screamed overgrown and out of control. The gardens were struggling to survive as invasive species had come in and declared war. A once-small grapevine lovingly planted for its bountiful fruit was tightly wrapped with weeds like a strait jacket. It wasn't a pretty sight.

Roxanne admitted she had not invited family or friends over for quite some time due to the state of her gardens. Aside from feeling overwhelmed and inundated, she was embarrassed. We will visit the notion of "letting go" a bit later, but I must express that we simply have to cut ourselves some slack, in and out of the gardens. Life happens while the rest of the world keeps spinning on its axis; our gardens (and weeds) do not stop either.

As Roxanne and I talked about a plan to reclaim her gardens, I watched her overwrought shoulders gradually relax. Tears of relief pooled in her eyes and we hugged. I knew just how she felt. We were kindred spirits. I explained the simple cardboard process I use for removing weeds and restoring gardens; we were going to bring back balance, ease and beauty – and the joy she once experienced with gardening. As I left, I assured her to not worry, help was on the way.

Roxanne's situation was the perfect candidate for successfully and organically eliminating an over-abundance of weeds. I have been using cardboard in gardens for years. Cardboard is plentiful, free and easy to use. It is the organic go-to solution to smother anything from weeds to sod.

Bonus: it acts as a natural weed barrier – and as it decomposes, it adds nutrients to the soil.

Here's how :

- ▶ **Weed control.** Now this is going to sound so easy because it is. Simply lay the cardboard over the weeds…yes, right over all the weeds. Do not, and I repeat, do not weed first. Lay a piece of cardboard, then add a thick layer of your favorite mulch, lay another piece of cardboard, and top again. Repeat this process until you have covered the weeds completely. Once the cardboard and top dressing are laid, spread evenly for a weed-free garden. Over time, the cardboard will slowly decompose while smothering the weeds. Underneath all the cardboard and mulch awaits organic compost ready for planting.

- ▶ **Weed prevention.** Cardboard is also a great weed *preventive* in the garden before you or someone else spreads mulch in your beds. Laying it earlier rather than later is a great way to reduce weeds all season long.

Gardens are meant to be a safe haven, not a place of bondage. Discovering ways to do things differently in life is a sign of strength. When I allow myself the opportunity to lessen a burden in one place it opens up new possibilities in another.

A valuable lesson I have learned through gardening is that Mother Nature is very merciful, even in the thick of a weedy garden bed. Let's face it; every now and again we need a little help in the garden and a whole lot of cardboard.

Weed Control #3:

A Bucket, Anyone?

My final contribution to create comfort and ease in the garden is sharing my Pink Bucket Chal-

lenge. Each day after work, I challenge myself to get in my gardens accompanied by a $5 pink bucket purchased at a local garage sale. My objective is two-fold: visit and weed my gardens daily without feeling inundated, while serving two important facets of life: my health and my gardens. Once my bucket is full, I retreat or not, the choice is mine. This stress-free and trouble-free practice gives me permission to do only what is reasonably required and expected; I set the parameter and expectation. This simple little ritual leaves me guilt-free and weed-free.

As I say so often, our gardens should be our love, not our labor of love. Perhaps you'll grab a bucket, fill it once or twice, and then retreat to your favorite garden chair. I believe it is just as important to be *present* in our gardens as it is to work in them.

ELEVEN

UNWANTED LAWN?

how to flip your sod and convert its rich soil into planting beds

The soil is the great connector of lives, the source and destination of all. It is the healer and restorer and resurrector, by which disease passes into health, age into youth, death into life. Without proper care for it we can have no community, because without proper care for it we can have no life.

~WENDELL BERRY

Driving a shovel or trowel into the soil can be a gardener's game changer. It can either entice you to dig deeper with enthusiasm or it can force you to grab your tools and run! It's all about having good soil to work with.

Case in Point

My client Michelle asked me to plant annuals in her large flowerbed. Her selection of purple Salvia, pink Begonia and white Alyssum was an excellent choice for her summer garden. Michelle said she did not have a green thumb, nothing grew for her, she loved flowers, but not gardening.

Not a problem; that's why I was here. The task sounded simple until I started digging my trowel into the soil and was met with much resistance. The soil was as hard as concrete, making the job impossible. I literally could not dig a three-inch hole, so I had to stop. No wonder Michelle was unsuccessful in the garden and gave up. Who wouldn't?

Healthy soil is critical to grow healthy plants. And so is a healthy (and happy) gardener. Digging in the soil with an acceptable amount of comfort and ease will ensure you and your plants come back for more!

I am a stickler about the soil I use for planting. Rich, organic soil is the cornerstone for healthy plants to thrive and grow. In my dedication to simplicity and ease, I have become a three-ingredient gardener:

▶ **Right plant, right place** (of course!)

▶ **Mulch for garden beds,** like shredded leaves, shredded hardwood or pine straw

▶ **Organic compost** (technically defined as decayed material used for planting and fertilizing). My definition of organic compost is black gold – it's a must-have!

A secret source of rich, rich soil. When you think about sources of good soil, do you ever think of your lawn? Most of us don't. In this chapter I'm going to focus on making the best use of the rich soil that already exists underneath the grassy surface of your lawn. It's called sod. In the next pages, I'm going to show you some very unconventional things to do with sod.

Did you know? One tablespoon of soil has more organisms in it than there are people on earth.

Repurposing the Soil Beneath Your Lawn

Do you have areas of lawn, or an entire lawn, that you would like to convert to planting beds? Lawns are anything but easy on the environment. They consume huge amounts of water and chemicals, they need constant maintenance and they are generally not good ambassadors of sustainability. Not only that, but removing a lawn and disposing of the sod can present environmental problems of their own. Most curbside city sanitation services will not haul it away in garbage cans, recycle bins or leaf bags. You could spend money to have a truck come and take it away, but it will end up in the landfill one way or another.

Is there a way to recycle sod that will save the landfill and at the same time help you to start a healthy new planting bed? Yes, indeed. If you're interested in a few out-of-the-box ways to lay fertile ground, read on. It could be a win-win solution.

Replacing your lawn with ornamental plants and shrubs means less work for you

Turning Lawn Into a Garden Bed: Flipping Sod

Here's the thing: you can recycle sod by simply flipping it over! Flipping it is a viable, sustainable and cost effective way to recycle sod. It's practical, economical and environmentally friendly.

When you turn a piece of sod over, you can see the thick, dark soil beneath. Now, imagine it turned grassy-side-down in a new planting bed, slowly decomposing into rich, nutrient-filled compost that naturally feeds and fertilizes plants. That's what's going to happen. Here's how to do it.

How to Remove Sod

Early disclaimer: I know I promised comfort and ease, but this is an exception. While the long-term payoff is in comfort and ease, flipping sod is laborious work; you may want to recruit or hire some help. Even if you cannot perform the physical task of flipping sod, why not instruct those who can?

A sod cutter is the most efficient tool for removing sod

The most efficient way to remove sod is with a motor-powered sod cutter. Many hardware or equipment rental stores rent them for a reasonable (and very worthwhile) fee. Sod cutters lift the sod like butter!

If a motor-powered sod cutter is unavailable, here is a way to manually remove sod: I use a half moon spade.

Begin by slicing/scoring the sod into small sections, dividing it like a grid. Smaller pieces make it easier to lift. Do not dig down too far; each section should be light enough to lift easily. Take your time. Removing sod manually is physical work; it takes muscle and patience. Call on family and friends to help, or hire a professional. Once the hard work is done, you have the joy of planting and attending to your new beautiful garden!

Creating a New Garden Bed for Flipped Sod

To prepare a new bed on a grassy area, you may need to remove the sod first and then add organic compost before planting. Don't let the initial work in creating a new garden deter you.

Outlining your bed line. Once you have designed your new garden and selected the right plants for the right place, it's time to create your bed line. Before removing the sod, use spray paint or a garden hose to lay out and define the new bed line. Bed lines form artistic curves and interest in the garden; aim for the right amount of flow. Straight bed lines can lack interest, too many winding curves can be hard to maintain, but the right amount of curves in a bed line can be very appealing.

Sod for Raised Beds

Raised gardens create an ideal environment for plants to thrive successfully. They allow for control over the soil and create the perfect planting medium with excellent drainage.

The flipping sod technique is a great way to build a raised garden. The sod reduces the amount of soil needed (and purchased) to raise up the bed, saving you money. Simply flip the sod over on the newly created garden bed, layer the sod like a pan of homemade lasagna, then backfill with your favorite organic soil. The flipped sod on the bottom of the pile will eventually decompose. It's so much better than trying to dispose of the sod!

Layer flipped sod to create raised beds

Two More Great Ways to Recycle Your Sod

- **As an excellent filler** in forgotten or neglected areas of the yard: Lay the sod (grassy side down) along the sides of a garage, along fence lines, house foundations, or over weedy garden beds. Once you've flipped the lawn, lay cardboard over it and then cover with mulch. For low spots in your lawn, remove the "old" stuff and patch the lawn with the "good" stuff (grass side up).

- **As a helpful "gift"** for your neighbors: Someone is always looking for extra sod to patch grass. Let neighbors know in advance that you are removing sod and are willing to recycle it to them. They'll be happy to reclaim it!

Extra sod can be given away

Or You Could Just Leave the Sod in Place...
and Create a New Garden Bed Right on Top!

If you are not up to the physical challenge of removing sod and are willing to be patient, you will love this technique. It's easy, inexpensive, and works very well. The very epitome of comfort and ease, relatively speaking. It involves some cardboard, mulch and then waiting for nature to do the rest. Sometimes it just makes sense to convert that unwanted area of lawn the simplest way imaginable.

- **First, design your new garden bed,** as discussed earlier. No changes there.
- **Next, collect free cardboard, lots of it.** Lay the cardboard, a few sheets at a time over the sod and dump a pile of mulch like shredded hardwood or pine straw (the choice is yours) on top of the cardboard, covering the sod.
- **Repeat this process** until the entire newly designated garden bed is full.
- **Here comes the hardest part: wait!** The sod is slowly decomposing under the cardboard and mulch.
- **A few months later,** push the mulch aside, plant, and re-cover with the mulch.

A Late Bloomer Memo:
It's okay to ask for help... that's what friends, relatives and landscape companies are for!

Removing, flipping or covering sod to create new beds will yield beautiful gardens

TWELVE

VEGGIES, FRUIT AND HERBS
feast and share with ease

᭗

*We're only secure when we look out our kitchen window
and see our food growing and our friends working nearby.*

~ BILL MOLLISON

I cannot think of two better things to celebrate in life than gardening and eating! In this chapter I'll share ways to reap (and eat) what you sow in the garden. I promise, I won't ask you to flip any more sod or haul barrows of compost. This will be all about nourishing your mind, body and soul with homegrown food!

Here's the good news: my cooking habits are similar to my gardening habits. In fact, if a recipe calls for more than five ingredients, I'm out. I'll recommend it to a friend and then invite myself to dinner. My edible gardening practices are even more laid back than my ornamental gardening ones. They go something like this:

▷ **Add organic soil**
▷ **Plant a plant**
▷ **Water**
▷ **Harvest**

It really can be that simple (and rewarding) if you set goals and boundaries before you dig in. I think we will all agree gardening and food go hand-in-hand, so I'm going to share some simple things to grow and enjoy in your kitchen from your garden. Without becoming overwhelmed.

Garden-to-table is rapidly gaining in popularity. A recent report found that 35% of all households in America are growing food at home or in a community garden – up 17% in five years.

Growing Your Own: Can You have Too Much of a Good Thing?

The rewards and benefits of growing food are too many to list…if you don't bite off more than you can chew, literally.

A Tale of Too Much

One spring, a very busy client, Sara, called because she wanted to start a vegetable garden just like her friends. A too-big veggie garden, I feared. I cautioned her about the size of the edible beds she was considering and suggested she start small, see how she likes farming, and then grow from there. Sara was highly motivated and anxious to get started so we forged ahead with her original plan.

Large gardens can be hard to maintain

Sod was removed and recycled, organic compost was spread and vegetable starters planted. By the end of the summer, Sara called again. The gardens were more than she could handle; keeping up with everything (including daily life) put her and her green thumb over the edge. She wanted other options but did not want to give up growing food.

My solution: I replaced most of Sara's struggling edibles with low maintenance shrubs and perennials and left a smaller area for Sara to grow vegetables, if she wanted.

My Small Garden

Like Sara, I love growing vegetables. Each season I harvest food from a small 4'x4' raised bed and a few patio containers. I learned my "go big or go home" lesson years ago. If there is something I want to eat but don't (won't or can't) grow, I visit my local farmers market; it is convenient and I love supporting them. It's the best of both worlds.

Raised beds are a convenient way to garden

I would never discourage someone from growing anything – hungry appetites are good. However, it is helpful to first consider how much you can and want to maintain before taking on too much. Having too much food is never the problem, though; there's always someone (human or animal) to share it with.

I believe gardening small is better than not gardening at all. If you overdo it the first time around like Sara, you may get a bad taste in your mouth (pun intended) and give up gardening altogether; and we don't want that to happen.

The Right-Size Edible Garden (for you)

Here are a few lessons I learned from others and from my own trials and errors:

- **Start small.** Bigger is not always better. You can expand your growing ambitions and your garden beds later – it's always an option.
- **Sow and grow only what you eat or can reliably give away or share.** It's important to consider whether or not the benefits outweigh the costs – remember, your labor is a "cost," also.

- **Raised garden beds make maintenance and harvesting easy** – the higher the bed the better. Why crawl around on your hands and knees if you don't have to? Raised beds also allow you to control the soil, which results in good drainage and healthy crops.

- **You don't need acres of land to grow food.** Containers and window boxes make excellent vessels to grown fruits and vegetables. You'd be surprised what you can grow in the smallest places.

- **Always expect someone (or something) other than you, your family and friends to nibble on your harvest,** because they (birds, squirrels, rabbits, etc.) will.

Grow herbs, fruit and vegetables in containers

Seedlings require time and care before they're planted in the garden

Starter plants, or from seed? Many gardeners like to sow their own seeds prior to the growing season; I prefer buying organic starter plants. I tried seeds a few times but felt the benefit did not outweigh the cost. However, I really love seed catalogs. Flipping pages of glorious flowers, vegetables, bulbs – you name it – certainly gets my garden juices flowing. Whichever option you choose (seeds or starter plant), you'll end up with delicious homegrown edibles.

My Top Easy Veggies

These will perform well and produce a generous harvest planted in a container, a raised bed or directly into the garden:

Green bell peppers

- **Bell Peppers:** Water pepper plants at the roots, not overhead. When it's time to harvest, cut off (don't pluck) the colorful fruit, leaving about one inch of the stem.

- **Cucumbers:** This is a great plant to grow on a trellis, especially if you need to save space. They are very easy to grow and produce a lot of fruit.

- **Eggplant:** Eggplant needs a sunny spot in your garden. It is not fond of cold and damp conditions.

Eggplant

- **Lettuce:** There's nothing better than lettuce from your garden, except perhaps tomatoes. Harvest by cutting at the base with a knife. I like to plant a few different varieties and create a true spring mix. Lettuce likes temperatures around 60°F - 65°F and prefers afternoon shade. Harvest your crop in the morning and eat the same day for ultimate freshness.

- **Pole Beans:** Harvest your beans often; they like to be "picked on" at least every few days. Beans like hot weather, so don't direct-sow seeds too early. Try to remove the dried beans; they discourage the plant from producing more.

- **Radishes:** Radishes love water and partial shade, which make them a perfect choice for a not-so-sunny spot in your garden. The tops are loaded with vitamins. The young, tender greens have a peppery flavor and are excellent in salads. Don't throw out the mature greens! Add them to your favorite soups and stews.

- **Spinach:** Harvest by cutting or pinching, never pulling. Spinach is considered a cold crop and can be planted in August, maturing in cooler temperatures. In hot/warm climates: plant in fall, harvest in winter and spring. In cold climates: plant in spring and August. Spinach is an excellent source of Vitamin K.

- **Swiss chard:** This plant loves organic compost as much as I do! When the chard gets six inches tall, don't cut – break with your hands. Chard makes a lovely border in the garden or mixed in a flowerbed or a container. Try planting Rainbow chard; it's not only tasty, it's oh-so pretty!

- **Tomatoes:** So many tomatoes, so little time! Did you know there are two types of tomatoes: indeterminate (vine) and determinate (bush)? I like planting both kinds for a little variety. General rule: plant two plants per person to ensure there's plenty to go around!

Tomatoes can be grown in a container or in the ground

Basic planting rules. The same planting rules for perennials, trees and shrubs apply to vegetable, fruits and herbs: read labels; right plant, right place. Edible plants grow and spread like ornamental plants. Keep your tape measure handy for placement and spacing. Remember: your best crop is your soil, so always use organic soil. You (and others) are eating your harvest. No pesticides or herbicides, please.

Give tomatoes plenty of room to grow in the garden

Raised Beds and Vertical Gardening

Raised bed and vertical gardening have gained popularity for many small space gardeners. And vertical gardening is a great way to grow up rather than out, requiring little space but adding wonderful interest to any wall.

There's no reason to bemoan the limitations of a small garden when you can grow something beautiful (or delicious) in containers of many kinds, in small raised beds, up a trellis against a patio wall…or simply drop a few tomato plants, chard and basil in among your ornamentals. Be like me: experiment, play and communicate with your plants!

Peas grow well on a vertical trellis

Foodscaping with Edibles and Ornamentals

Mixing edibles and ornamentals in landscapes and gardens looks gorgeous and is extremely wise and efficient if you have limited space. Kale, Swiss chard, cabbage, and lettuce (to name a few) make fabulous garden borders and are very attractive in mixed containers with your favorite summer annuals and perennials.

Growing Fruit

Backyard gardeners are not just growing vegetables, they're growing fruit, too. In fact, I designed a front garden that included four columnar apple and pear trees. Columnar varieties grow up instead of out, and from 8 to 10 feet tall and 3 to 4 feet wide. How cool is that? Small fruit trees and shrubs are ideal for urban plots or suitable containers. Blueberries, blackberries, raspberries and currants are among some of the most popular fruits to grow because they are easy to maintain and harvest. Bonus: not only are fruit bearing trees and shrubs delicious and practical, they are very attractive in the garden. And don't forget strawberries! With a little research, you can grow mouth-watering fruits in your outdoor space, big or small. Just be prepared to share and share alike with the wildlife.

Berries such as these luscious blackberries, blueberries and raspberries are easy to grow in the garden

Herbs for Good Taste and Good Health

Growing herbs is easy and fun. There's nothing like freshly cut herbs from your garden. Not only are herbs wonderful to use in the kitchen, they have many medicinal values, too.

My friend Lisa Steele is my go-to expert on growing and using herbs. She lives and gardens in Maine. Lisa is the author of *Fresh Eggs Daily* and *Duck Eggs Daily*. I asked her what she likes best about growing herbs for her family and her flock. Here's what Lisa had to say:

As I get older, I find myself growing more herbs and fewer vegetables. Herbs are so forgiving. They don't really care what kind of soil you plant them in, if you fertilize them or even if you remember to water them. They produce for you all summer long – and they're easy to dry for use through the winter. And many are perennials so you only have to plant them once and they come back year after year. That's my favorite kind of gardening!

Herbs for Cooking

Following is a list of my favorite easy-to-grow herbs, with helpful information to get you started. Some of these delightful cooking herbs are also part of Mother Nature's medicine chest. Later in the chapter you'll find a list of my favorite medicinal herbs and what they're good for. But for now, herbs for cooking:

Sweet basil

- **Sweet Basil (Ocimum basilicum):** Plant in full sun, well-drained soil. Pruning: pinch off the center shoot so it does not flower (pinching helps to encourage new leaves). If it does go to flower, no worries, just pinch it off. Clip a big bunch of basil and put it in a vase of water on your kitchen counter. I love how it smells indoors!

- **Parsley (Petroselinium crispum):** I prefer Italian flat-leaf parsley for no other reason than I like the taste. Parsley likes rich, moist soil and prefers full to part sun. When you are ready to harvest your crop, simply snip what you need with a scissors or cut back at the base.

- **Dill (Anethum graveolens):** Plant dill in full sun with rich, well-drained soil. Harvest by cutting off the leaves with a scissors.

- **Rosemary (Rosmarinus officinalis):** Rosemary loves full sun and well-drained soil. It is used as a shrub in dry climates and mild summers, like California and Texas. In colder temperatures, grow rosemary in a container – it is not winter hardy.

- **Sage (Salvia offficinalis):** Sage loves dry, well-drained soil. Like rosemary, sage is a shrub (evergreen) used in the Mediterranean and southeastern Europe.

- **Common Thyme (Thymus vulgaris):** This classic herb is great in the kitchen and in the garden. Thyme makes a lovely scented ground cover and is so easy to grow. This plant does best in full sun and prefers light, well-drained soil. I have thyme growing in my "hell-strip" along with other perennials next to my sidewalk – it looks really beautiful when it blooms and smells heavenly for those walking by.

Herbs for Health

Growing herbs for medicinal purposes offer many benefits and make excellent home-made remedies. Here are a few of my favorite herbs to grow that have long-reputed healing properties. (*Note:* I'm not a physician, so I can't make any medical claims, except to say how these herbs have been used for generations and centuries all over the world to address varied health conditions).

Swallowtail caterpillar munching on parsley

- **Parsley (*Petroselinium crispum*):** Top to bottom, this herb will refresh your breath and help with flatulence. Double your pleasure and double your fun!

- **Sage (*Salvia offficinalis*):** Sage gives relief for inflammation in your mouth or throat.

- **Common Thyme (*Thymus vulgaris*):** This herb is an antiseptic and ideal for coughs and congestion.

- **Lavender (*Lavandula* species):** Stop and smell the lavender! It's ideal for calming and relaxing your nerves.

- **Pot Marigold (*Calendula offficinalis*):** Too much sun from gardening? Marigold is good for sunburns and other skin abrasions or infections.

- **Lemon Balm (*Melissa officinalis*):** The Jack-of-all-trades! Lemon balm relieves wounds, anxiety, insect bites, and much more. I recommend planting lemon balm in a container; it likes to wander around the garden too much.

- **St. John's Wort (*Hypericum perforatum*):** The leaves and flowers of St. John's wort are often used for depression. This deciduous shrub is very attractive in the landscape.

- **Rosemary (*Rosmarinus officinalis*):** Feeling grumpy? Rosemary will lift your mood. It can also help with memory.

- **Sweet Violet (*Viola odorata*):** Chronic skin problems like eczema? Let sweet violet get a jump on it – internally and topically.

Blooming Edibles

Petals-to-Table

A flower is not just a pretty face or somewhere to stick your nose. For a very long time (maybe forever) flowers have made their way into the kitchens of diverse cultures and heritages. Flowers not only fancy up a dinner plate or summer salad, they add unique flavors to many recipes and cuisines.

A word of caution: not all flowers are created equal or are edible. Always eat only the flowers you grow. Here's why: you don't want to take a chance and eat flowers that have been treated with anything toxic, like herbicides and pesticides. And remove pistils (the female reproductive part of a flower) and stamens (the male reproductive organ of a flower) before cooking or consuming – the flower may not be as tasty otherwise, and more importantly: for those with allergies, the pollen may cause an allergic reaction.

Planning a brunch or dinner gathering? Add a little pizzazz, color and flavor to your guest list and menu. Bon appétit!

Eat this Flower	Not this Flower
Bee Balm: Minty flavor	Anemone
Clover: Sweet with a bit of licorice	Azalea
Daylily: Asparagus flavor	Buttercup
Dianthus: Sweet	Clematis
Hollyhock: Showier than tasty	Daffodils
Lavender: Sweet and spicy	Delphinium
Nasturtium: Sweet, floral and spicy all in one	Foxglove
Pansy: Wintergreen flavor	Hydrangea
Rose: Perfumed flavor	Iris
Scented Geranium	Lily-of-the-Valley
Squash Blossom: Squash flavor	Monkshood
Hibiscus: Cranberry flavor	Oleander
Jasmine: Fragrant and pretty	Sweet Pea
Violet: Sweet tasting	Wisteria

Growing and Sharing: Neighborhood CSA's

My friend Jill Plum is from California and is the founder and CEO of Art in the Garden (gorgeous raised beds from 100% recycled metal). Jill rocks at growing edibles. She has a lot of knowledge and experience with Community Sustainable Agriculture. CSA's are great options and resources for those with little space but who still want to share and grow homegrown edibles. CSA's can be any size, from farms to a group of neighbors who share their bounty with one another.

Jill's local CSA is made up of 14 front yard and back yard gardens – with what she describes as "an astounding variety of flowers, herbs and vegetables growing side by side, encouraging pollinators to visit." Maintenance is done by homeowners and the CSA leaders. At harvest time, the bounty is gathered and shared with all 14 households. It is truly a community effort and blessing. Find out more about CSA's at www.localharvest.org.

THIRTEEN

PERFECTLY IMPERFECT
relaxing and letting go

❦

Each day, awakening, are we asked to paint the sky blue?
Need we coax the sun to rise or flowers to bloom?
Need we teach birds to sing, or children to laugh, or lovers to kiss?
No, though we think the world imperfect, it surrounds us each day
with its perfections. We are asked only to appreciate them,
and to show appreciation by living in peaceful harmony amidst them.
The Creator does not ask that we create a perfect world;
He asks that we celebrate it.

~ ROBERT BRAULT

As you've seen, *Late Bloomer* isn't a conventional how-to gardening book. Far from it. That wasn't really my point in writing it. There is a wealth of gardening information to be had and it can be mind boggling. Early on in my gardening life, I tried to learn and remember everything. Heck, I even tried making up my own words and rules. I don't do that anymore; now, I keep things simple and organic. It's easier that way. I no longer compromise my limitations; it's too stressful. I've set boundaries in the kitchen and in the garden. Thank goodness my gardening skills are way more developed than my cooking skills — we are all a work in progress, right? But my point is, and will always be, that gardening should be a soulful, satisfying experience, yours to create in a way that connects you with Mother Nature in all her amazing guises. I like to say it's the fine art of soul to soil.

Chasing Perfection

One of my favorite gardens to tend is very small in size and very formal, and belongs to my client Sharron. The gardens are not my personal style but I love them for their simple elegance. Tall, stately Arborvitaes line the perimeter and serve as a natural screening for privacy. 'Annabelle' Hydrangeas create a soft, luxurious feel against the deep green Arborvitae. Neatly hedged Boxwoods in front of the Hydrangeas give the gardens a well-manicured appearance. The three-tiered gardens are stunning, especially when the Hydrangeas are in full bloom. To top it off, right smack in the middle was a lovely petite white Kousa Dogwood tree. The plant selections were lovely —

perfect for a formal garden. Unfortunately, Mother Nature's ways are not, and the once-attractive Dogwood died from a harsh winter not long ago. So I was on a '"tree hunt" for the perfect replacement.

My client and I decided on a new species, size and branch structure as a replacement. The new tree had to be perfect. I spent many hours shopping, but to my surprise, not one met our demands. Each time I thought I came close to finding an ideal replacement, I'd call my client and she'd ask, "Is it perfect?" It never was. None measured up to our expectations, so my search continued. It's been a while now, and the tree has yet to be replaced.

It's hard to find a perfect tree; nature is not flawless (according to our human expectations). I think nature is perfectly imperfect. Through that experience, I learned there is no such thing as perfect – not in life, not in nature, and not in the garden. But I believe when you take unrealistic expectations out of gardening, new possibilities emerge, like relaxing and letting go. I hope you can let go of the pressure to conform or produce, or be perfect, and find your own hardiness zone in life, your place of balance and harmony.

I think about this idea of perfection a lot as I tend the gardens of others as well as my own. Many of the old Masters believed that there was no such thing as a perfect painting or a finished work of art. And so they would leave some part of it unfinished, sometimes with a small "flaw" that only they could notice. In the East, the Japanese express art and design through the concept of *wabi-sabi* (roughly translated as quietness, simplicity, impermanence). In *wabi-sabi* nothing is perfect or even finished, and yet that very quality is what gives it its unique character and warmth. You can see it in the classic Japanese gardens that convey a feeling of calm and flow, rather than rigidity and conclusion.

A garden is never finished, and neither are we. How wonderful! ❧

The Other Woman with a Hoe

People often ask me about the name of my garden business, Two Women and a Hoe. Who is the second woman? I'd like you to meet her.

My mother has always been my inspiration. She was an incredible entrepreneur, a business owner, and one of the smartest people you could meet. Two Women and a Hoe is a tribute to her memory.

My mother was not a gardener and, unlike me, did not enjoy digging in the soil or getting dirty. Her kitchen was her garden where plenty of homemade Italian meals were prepared and enjoyed. But each summer my mother planted a row of red petunias in our brick flowerbox next to the porch. It was a staple in our sparse urban landscape.

The yearly planting of perky red petunias by my mother marked the start of long-anticipated summer vacations; happy times for everyone. Then the dog days of summer set in and my mother's gardening enthusiasm wilted like the once-adored petunias. No one ever spoke about the leafless flowers. Their remains simply lay there in the dried soil, unattended. At season's end, they quietly disappeared.

How the petunias made their way to the flowerbox or how they were planted does not matter; the memories and efforts of my mother do matter. Her lifeless petunias may have been controverial around the neighborhood but her drive and spirit never wavered. My mother planted other valuable seeds in my life. I can't help but wonder (and giggle to myself) if those silly petunias are the direct root of my love and passion for gardening today.

So, yes, the "other woman" is my mother. Now, this is going to sound strange, but the other woman is also my brother, Michael, whose sudden death in 2006 caused me to reevaluate my life path and trade in my corporate heels for my Wellies.

The other woman might be you, too. Whether you're male or female, you may feel like I did. Know that I know you; you inspire me with your desire to identify your passion. I say, you can figure out what your "Wellies" are, whether you are in the garden or not!

I want to close by mentioning another artist whose work I adore, the American painter Georgia O'Keeffe. She held her own until she left us at age 98. O'Keeffe stayed true to herself and her work. She knew her comfort (hardiness) zone in life. You have probably seen her extraordinary paintings from nature. Her Petunia series is my favorite because it reminds me of my mother and my childhood.

If you are not familiar with O'Keeffe's work, I encourage you to check her out. I think you will enjoy her as much as I do. You can view her paintings at www.okeeffemuseum.org.

I'll let Georgia O'Keeffe send us into our gardens with these words:

When you take a flower in your hand and really look at it,
it's your world for the moment. I want to give that world to someone else.
Most people in the city rush around so, they have no time to look at a flower.

❧

Please stay in touch. I want to hear about your garden successes, experiments, tips, what works for you and what doesn't. It's been a pleasure sharing my gardening life with you and I'm honored to include you in my Two Women and a Hoe family. Thank you for picking up this book!

Organic Garden Remedies from My Online Community

※

Imentioned early on that I learn organic garden recipes from friends and other gardeners. I also get the very best organic remedies from my beloved Two Women and a Hoe Facebook Friends. Whenever I need something or have a question, I ask and they deliver! These gardeners have been there, done that in more ways than one! I admire them because they love organic gardening as much as I do. They know how to get things done without harming the environment. What's not to love?

I am so excited to share some of these "unedited" homemade organic remedies from the finest gardeners in the country:

Aphids

▷ *Garlic water to kill aphids.* ~ Lisa B.

Deer deterrent

▷ *You can easily make your own. Take organic dormant oil and simmer it for a couple hours with a whole bulb of crushed garlic. Seal it in a jar and let it infuse for a week or two, then strain out the garlic pieces and mix with water per oil label instructions to spray.*
~ Lynn L.

Insect and pest control

▷ *I make my own insecticidal soap with original Dawn dishwashing liquid soap and lots of water. I also use white vinegar to kill weeds coming out off sidewalk cracks, etc.* ~ Kim M.

- *I spray leaves with a mix of Castile soap and water to keep unwanted pests down without harming my little helpers (little people and helpful insects).* ~ Ona W.

- *I use cayenne pepper to help control insects.* ~ Kitty H.

- *Rhubarb leaves mashed in boiling soapy dishwater, strained and cooled: a great organic pest control for potato beetles, aphids and ants, etc. (Don't spray on vegetable foliage if you plan to eat the foliage.)* ~ Sandy G.

- *I use a blend of whatever herbs I have in the garden (NOT Stevia – do not use anything sweet to attract the pests). I boil the herbal blend in water; take off the heat, let steep for about 2-3 hours (depending on my schedule) and strain. I put it in a sprayer and spray daily on all my veggies, flowers and Hostas. You can always add a bit of cayenne (a bit).* ~ Gwen M.

- *Chickens are natural bug killers.* ~ Jane M.

- *I use many pest controls. My favorite last year was a strip of wood (8" x 3") with top part painted a bright yellow, then coated with petroleum jelly. Place unpainted section into the ground around plants It caught many a cabbage moth among a few other insects. Recoat as needed.* ~ Janet M.

- *For roses: I cut up a bar of Ivory soap and stick it in the ground around the roses. The leaves are never bitten by insects. This really works.* ~ Linnie H.

Planting

- *Epsom salt in the garden, crushed egg shells and coffee grounds, too."* ~ Julie L.

- *You can't beat horse manure tea for making plants grow! We live in a southwestern Ontario, Canada, community close to Amish and Mennonite families, so horse manure is plentiful.* ~ Wayne S.

- *Composted horse manure as a manure tea.* ~ Julie L.

- *We make our own compost from our cow manure for five years now…BEST gardens I have ever had. When it's matured, its consistency is just like potting soil. We use no chemicals in our garden. We have no bug problems.* ~ Kenneth D.

Tomatoes

▶ *Use egg shells and coffee grounds for the tomatoes.*
~ Susan C.

▶ *We always plant our fish scraps next to our tomato plants after we fillet our catch in the summer. You have to go a shovel deep so the neighborhood cats don't dig them up. Our families always did this for great tomatoes.* ~ Judy B.

▶ *To prevent blossom-end rot, I use eggshells when I plant my tomatoes. But a few years ago when I dug up plants at season's end, I noticed that the shells were often still in large pieces – they take too long to break down! So now I throw all the shells in a canister to dry out, and when it's full, I powder the shells with a coffee grinder. Easy storing. When planting tomatoes I add a tablespoon to the hole. When blooms start to set, I sprinkle another tablespoon around each plant and water in.* ~ Lynn L.

▶ *To pollinate tomatoes in the absence of bees: Use Q-tips to swab gently inside blossom and transfer pollen to another.* ~ Kimberly J.

Weed control

▶ *Use the pickling juices from your household uses and your dishwater: strain through a cheese cloth and spray on your weeds. All the vinegar salt and soap are at no additional cost to you.* ~ Sandy G.

▶ *Homemade lard soap, dissolved in water with vinegar for weed control. Without the vinegar and salt, it can also discourage some insects that feed on garden plants – I guess it smells a little bit "animal."* ~ Lynn L.

▶ *Vinegar and salt for weeds and invasive plants.* ~ Julie L.

▶ *For weeds in cracks, I put salt on weeds in my brick walkways or paver areas. Also make a spray of vinegar, salt and water to apply to weeds. I've heard that salt will damage cement, though.* ~ Wendy W.

▶ *We use white vinegar alone for the weeds and it works very well, that way it won't damage your cement.* ~ Sally C.

Acknowledgments

⌘

First, I want to thank my husband, Walter, for his continued support, especially when I started my landscape business. Thank you for not thinking I was crazy when I bought my first work truck off eBay for $2,800.00 (sight unseen), and for driving me across the state to pick it up. Thank you for lifting me up (literally) after a hard day's work in the garden, suggesting I take a hot shower and eat something because tomorrow would be better. Tomorrow was always better (and easier) because of your love and support.

To my wonderful mother-in-law and father-in-law, Mr. and Mrs. Arthur Bills – thank you for giving me the best gift ever, your adorable, caring son. The apple did not fall far from the tree.

Thanks to my loving and generous parents for teaching me that hard work pays off. You were always right, even when I thought you weren't. A special thanks to my brother Michael who assured me that "can't never could." May you all rest in peace and know that a day does not go by that I don't think of you.

To my dear friends Linda Johnson, Dawna Tennant and Denise Tucker – thank you for your gift of friendship, love and support. Linda, you are my spiritual compass and favorite art historian. Dawna, you are my true soil sister who loves getting dirty too; and Denise, you and I go way back and for that I am grateful.

To my St. Lynn's Press Family – many thanks to Paul, Cathy, Holly and Chloe. You are the finest, most dedicated team of professionals; it has been an honor working with you. Thank you for taking a chance on me, I will appreciate this opportunity forever. Cathy, you are an editing guardian angel sent from heaven. Holly, you are a creative genius!

About the Author

Jan Coppola Bills is a certified landscape designer, advanced master gardener, entrepreneur, and contributing writer for *State-by-State Gardening* magazine. She holds a masters degree in Organizational Management. After a successful career in the corporate world, she made a major life reassessment and followed her heart: She traded in her heels for Wellies and started the Detroit-area landscape design company Two Women and a Hoe (twowomenandahoe.com). Jan shares her gardening philosophy of comfort, ease and simplicity with her clients, in her speaking engagements, and with her large online community on Facebook, Twitter, Instagram, LinkedIn and Pinterest.

Index

Index

OTHER BOOKS FROM ST. LYNN'S PRESS

www.stlynnspress.com

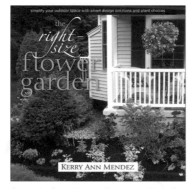

The Right-Size Flower Garden
by Kerry Mendez
160 pages • Hardback • ISBN: 978-0-9892688-7-5

The Cocktail Hour Garden
by C.L. Fornari
160 pages • Hardback • ISBN: 978-0-9892688-0-6

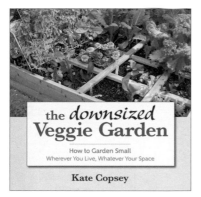

The Downsized Veggie Garden
by Kate Copsey
160 pages • Hardback • ISBN: 978-1-9433660-0-2

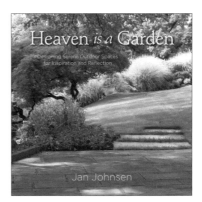

Heaven is a Garden
by Jan Johnsen
160 pages • Hardback • ISBN: 978-0-9855622-9-8